# The Pampered Chef

# Delightful Desserts
## From Easy to Elegant

Everybody loves dessert! Whether it's a decadent chocolate creation, homey fruit cobbler, dreamy cream pie or giant cookie chock-full of nuts and candies, we all look forward to a homemade dessert or special sweet treat. At The Pampered Chef Test Kitchens we love desserts too, so it gives us great pleasure to share our favorites with you in our cookbook, *Delightful Desserts*.

We hope you will enjoy cooking from this book. There's a chapter devoted to easy desserts, with recipes that use many convenience products, and one that specializes in spectacular sweets for special occasions. We offer a chapter of comfort desserts for brightening family mealtimes, while the last chapter features portable treats just perfect for toting to casual parties, neighborhood potlucks and school bake sales.

In *Delightful Desserts*, we provide clearly written recipes in numbered steps with enticing color photographs. The time required for preparing, baking and cooling each dessert is provided, along with expanded nutritional information. Finally, there are special Kitchen Tips to help you make the most of your Pampered Chef stoneware, cookware and tools. So, we encourage you to gather family and friends to share these delightful desserts, and wish you many sweet memories.

Enjoy!

*The Pampered Chef Test Kitchens*

# Contents

## Sweet and Simple ....4

### Time-Saving Treats
### for Today's Busy Lifestyles

Even when time is short, you can treat family and friends to delicious homemade desserts. It's all possible with our fast-to-fix recipes and convenience products such as cake and pudding mixes, refrigerated doughs, packaged cookies, ice creams and frozen whipped topping. What's more, these recipes have just 3-7 ingredients, so your shopping list is always short. With Pampered Chef recipes and tools, you can surprise your children with *Peanut Butter Blossoms* or delight guests with *Grasshopper Dessert Squares*, even when life is hectic. Just remember, take time for the compliments.

*Angel Almond Macaroons, Strawberry Ice p. 29*

## Dessert Classics .....34

### Traditional Favorites with
### Timeless Appeal

Streusel-topped apple pies, juicy sweet peach cobblers and chewy oatmeal cookies— everyone loves these old-fashioned goodies. And while there's nothing quite as satisfying as these time-honored classics, we've added flavor twists and timesaving tips to create our best-ever collection of comfort desserts. From our Test Kitchens to your home kitchen, we offer *Triple Berry Cherry Pie, Caramel Pecan Bread Pudding, Pineapple Upside-Down Cake* and many more, all baked to perfection in our Pampered Chef Stoneware and Cookware.

*Quick Carrot Cake p. 43*

*Coconut Cake p. 72*

# Desserts with Drama....64

*Dazzling, Delicious and
Decadent Delights*

Fancy cream pies, tender puff pastries and sensuous chocolate creations star in this wonderful chapter of elegant desserts. We've designed a dessert menu that combines the perfect Pampered Chef tools, convenience products and creative techniques to produce dramatic results. Key lime pie comes with a buttery macadamia nut crust. A pretty, pink lemonade dessert is sweet and refreshing, and a delightfully guilt-free choice. And when it's time to indulge, we tempt you with *New York-Style Cheesecake* or *Decadent Chocolate Cake*. Whatever the occasion, you deserve a most elegant ending.

# Treats that Travel ........96

*Crowd-Pleasing Desserts for
Parties, Picnics and Potlucks*

When it's your turn to bring the sweets, look to this chapter of tempting treats. We guarantee they'll deliver on taste and portability. Heading to the neighborhood picnic? *Black Forest Trifle* and *Summer Fruit Sampler* stay chilled even during warm summer months with the help of our special Chillzanne® serving products. Baking for a crowd? Turn to recipes for chocolate sheet cake, gooey nut bars or crispy cracker confections—all made in our large Stoneware Bar Pan. From classroom snacks to potluck pleasers, count on The Pampered Chef for imaginative recipe ideas and quality kitchen tools.

*Triple Layer Brownies p. 104*

# Sweet and Simple

### Time-Saving Treats for Today's Busy Lifestyles

*Grasshopper Dessert Squares p. 6*

**Prep time: 15 minutes**
**Cool time: 1 hour**
**Freeze time: 6 hours or overnight**

### Cook's Tip

▲ Mint chocolate chip ice cream can be substituted for vanilla ice cream; omit peppermint extract. Prepare as recipe directs.

### Tool Tips

▲ When making crumb crusts for desserts, you'll find the **Food Chopper** is a great tool for chopping graham crackers and cookies, especially creme-filled sandwich cookies.

▲ To garnish dessert squares, use the **Crinkle Cutter** to cut cookies in half. The Crinkle Cutter is a handy tool when making ice cream sundaes for a party. Cut the container away from a 1/2-gallon block of ice cream, then cut ice cream into cubes. Toppings will stay put in the ridges made by the Crinkle Cutter.

# Grasshopper Dessert Squares

*Pictured on p. 4*
*With hectic schedules, frozen desserts are the answer.*
*This yummy chocolate-mint dessert can be made days before you need to serve it.*

21   **fudge mint cookies (1¼ cups finely chopped)**
 1   **tablespoon butter or margarine, melted**
 1   **quart vanilla ice cream**
 1   **container (8 ounces) frozen whipped topping, thawed, divided**
¼   **teaspoon peppermint extract**
 4   **drops green food coloring (optional)**
     **Additional fudge mint cookies, cut in half (optional)**
     **Fresh mint leaves (optional)**

1. Preheat oven to 350°F. Finely chop cookies using **Food Chopper**; place in **Small Batter Bowl**. Add butter; mix well. Press crumb mixture onto bottom of **Square Baker**. Bake 8 minutes. Cool completely.

2. Place ice cream in refrigerator for 20 minutes to soften. Chill **Classic Batter Bowl** in refrigerator at the same time. Place Baker with cooled crust in freezer.

3. Scoop ice cream into chilled Batter Bowl. Stir until softened and blended; gently fold in 2 cups of the whipped topping, peppermint extract and food coloring, if desired. Spread ice cream mixture evenly over cold crust. Cover with aluminum foil; freeze 6 hours or overnight.

4. When ready to serve, let stand at room temperature 10 minutes. Attach open star tip to **Easy Accent® Decorator**; fill with remaining whipped topping. Cut dessert into squares with knife dipped in warm water. Garnish each square with remaining whipped topping. Add cookie half and mint leaves, if desired.

Yield: 9 servings

Nutrients per serving: Calories 240, Total Fat 13 g, Saturated Fat 9 g, Cholesterol 30 mg, Carbohydrate 28 g, Protein 3 g, Sodium 105 mg, Fiber less than 1 g
Diabetic exchanges per serving: 1 Starch, 1 Fruit, 2½ Fat (2 Carb, 2 Fat)

# Harvest Spiced Nuts

*Pictured on p. 8*

*These crunchy spiced pecans are addictive. Packaged in a festive container, they make a welcomed hostess gift, especially during the holiday season.*

1  egg, separated
1  package (8 ounces) pecan halves
½  cup packed brown sugar
½  teaspoon Pantry Cinnamon Plus™ Spice Blend

1. Preheat oven to 350°F. Line **Stoneware Bar Pan** with an 11-inch piece of **Parchment Paper**. Using **Egg Separator**, separate egg into **Classic Batter Bowl**. (Reserve yolk for another use.) Whip egg white using Egg Separator until frothy.

2. Add pecans to Batter Bowl. Toss to coat evenly with egg white using **Mix 'N Scraper®**. Sprinkle brown sugar and Spice Blend over pecans; toss to coat evenly. Pour pecans out onto parchment, separating into a single layer.

3. Bake 18-20 minutes or until nuts begin to brown. Remove pan from oven. Carefully slide parchment with pecans onto **Nonstick Cooling Rack**. Cool completely. Place in serving dish. Serve using **Small Serving Tongs**.

Yield: 4 cups

Nutrients per serving (¼ cup): Calories 130, Total Fat 10 g, Saturated Fat 1 g, Cholesterol 0 mg, Carbohydrate 9 g, Protein 2 g, Sodium 5 mg, Fiber less than 1 g
Diabetic exchanges per serving (¼ cup): ½ Starch, 2 Fat (½ Carb, 2 Fat)

## Kitchen Tips

**Prep time:** 5 minutes
**Bake time:** 18-20 minutes
**Cool time:** 20 minutes

### Cook's Tips

▲ Store *Harvest Spiced Nuts* in a tightly covered container at room temperature.

▲ These nuts are a delicious topping for scoops of ice cream, especially ice cream that's on top of apple pie. Or, add to a dollop of whipped cream on pumpkin pie.

▲ Substitute pumpkin pie spice for Cinnamon Plus™ Spice Blend, if desired.

# Quick Chocolate-Mint Fudge

*Imagine making fudge that's ready to eat in just 40 minutes.*
*Our Chillzanne® Platter makes it possible.*

1 package (8 ounces) semi-sweet chocolate squares for baking, divided

1 package (6 ounces) white chocolate squares for baking

1 container (16 ounces) prepared vanilla frosting, divided

1/4 teaspoon peppermint or mint extract

3 drops green or red food coloring

1/2 teaspoon vegetable oil

1. Using **Crinkle Cutter**, coarsely chop semi-sweet and white chocolate squares, keeping each separate. Reserve 1/2 cup of the semi-sweet chocolate for garnishing. Cut two 12-inch squares of **Parchment Paper**. Place one parchment square on chilled **Chillzanne® Platter**.

2. Combine white chocolate and half of the frosting in **Small (2-qt.) Saucepan**. Stir over low heat until melted and smooth. Add peppermint extract and food coloring; mix well. Pour mixture onto Chillzanne® Platter; spread into an 8-inch square. Let stand 5 minutes until mixture begins to set.

3. Meanwhile, in same saucepan, combine semi-sweet chocolate and remaining frosting. Stir over low heat until melted and smooth. Carefully pour chocolate mixture over mint layer on Chillzanne® Platter; spread evenly to cover mint layer using **Large Spreader**. Let stand 10 minutes to set.

4. Lay remaining parchment square over top of fudge. Smooth top by gently rolling **Baker's Roller™** over parchment. Lift up fudge with the aid of the parchment paper and turn over. Carefully peel parchment off mint layer of fudge.

5. For garnish, place reserved 1/2 cup chopped chocolate and oil in **Small Micro-Cooker®**. Microwave, uncovered, on HIGH 1-1 1/2 minutes or until melted, stirring every 30 seconds. Drizzle chocolate over fudge. Refrigerate until firm, 15-30 minutes. Place parchment with fudge on **Cutting Board**. Cut into 1-inch squares. Store in tightly covered container in refrigerator.

Yield: 64 squares

Nutrients per serving (1 square): Calories 60, Total Fat 3.5 g, Saturated Fat 1.5 g, Cholesterol 0 mg, Carbohydrate 8 g, Protein 0 g, Sodium 15 mg, Fiber 0 g
Diabetic exchanges per serving (1 square): 1/2 Fruit, 1/2 Fat (1/2 Carb, 1/2 Fat)

## Kitchen Tips

**Prep, cook and cool time: 40 minutes**

### Cook's Tips

▲ It's really not necessary to wash the saucepan between heating the two chocolate mixtures. Always keep in mind that a single drop of water added to melted chocolate can cause the chocolate to clump and harden.

▲ To drizzle melted chocolate for garnish, place a small plastic bag over rim of **Measure-All® Cup**, with one corner pointing down into the cup. Pour melted chocolate mixture into bag. Remove bag, twist top and secure with **Twixit! Clip**. Cut a very small piece off corner of bag to drizzle chocolate.

### Tool Tip

▲ It's important to freeze the **Chillzanne® Platter** at least 4 hours before preparing this recipe.

# Citrus Striped Angel Cake

*We've trimmed down the ingredient list, calories and fat in this carefree, guilt-free delightful dessert.*

1 package (16 ounces) angel food cake mix
1 package (0.3 ounce) sugar-free orange gelatin
3/4 cup boiling water
1/2 cup cold water
2 cups thawed, frozen light whipped topping
1 orange (optional)
1/2 pint raspberries (optional)
   Fresh mint leaves (optional)

1. Preheat oven to 350°F. Prepare cake mix according to package directions. Pour batter into ungreased **Rectangular Baker**, spreading evenly. Bake on center rack in oven 35-40 minutes or until top is golden brown and cracks feel dry and not sticky. (Cake should be firm to the touch; do not underbake.) Carefully turn Baker upside down onto **Nonstick Cooling Rack**; cool 45 minutes. (Do not remove cake from Baker.)

2. Using **Nylon Fork** or metal skewer, poke holes in cake about 1 1/2 inches deep and 1/2 inch apart.

3. Place gelatin in **Small Batter Bowl**. Pour boiling water into gelatin; stir about 2 minutes or until completely dissolved. Stir in cold water. Slowly pour gelatin evenly over cake. Refrigerate 3 hours.

4. Frost cake with whipped topping using **Large Spreader**. Cut into squares. Garnish each serving with orange slice, orange zest, raspberries and mint leaves, if desired.

Yield: 15 servings

LOW FAT Nutrients per serving: Calories 140, Total Fat 1 g, Saturated Fat 1 g, Cholesterol 0 mg, Carbohydrate 28 g, Protein 3 g, Sodium 240 mg, Fiber 0 g
Diabetic exchanges per serving: 1 Starch, 1 Fruit (2 Carb)

## Kitchen Tips

Prep time: 20 minutes
Bake time: 35-40 minutes
Cool time: 45 minutes
Chill time: 3 hours

### Cook's Tips

▲ To make holes in cake 1 1/2 inches deep, wrap a piece of transparent tape around tines of the **Nylon Fork**, 1 1/2 inches from ends of tines. Insert fork in cake just to the edge of the tape.

▲ For a pretty garnish, use the Lemon Zester/Scorer to zest the orange before cutting it into slices. Starting at the stem end, firmly draw the Lemon Zester/Scorer down along the skin of the orange to create long strips of peel. Repeat around whole orange then cut orange crosswise into 8 slices. Cut slices in half.

### Tool Tip

▲ To cut easily through angel food cake, use a gentle sawing motion with the **Serrated Bread Knife**.

**Prep time:** 10 minutes
**Bake time:** 10-12 minutes per batch
**Cool time:** 20 minutes

### Cook's Tip

▲ Chocolate kisses should be completely set before storing cookies. If you're in a hurry, once the cookies have cooled, place them in the refrigerator for a few minutes to set the chocolates.

### Tool Tips

▲ Use the **Medium Scoop** to fill the barrel of the **Cookie Press** with cookie dough.

▲ To begin pressing cookie dough, squeeze lower trigger twice; there will be two clicks. If dough does not begin extruding through the disk then squeeze twice again. Pull Cookie Press straight up. Re-position cookie press and squeeze trigger once; pull Cookie Press straight up. Repeat the one squeeze method until Baking Stone is full.

# Peanut Butter Blossoms

*With our Cookie Press and convenient refrigerated dough, cookie making can't get any easier, or more fun!*

1   **package (18 ounces) refrigerated sugar cookie dough**
1/2  **cup creamy peanut butter**
42  **milk chocolate candy kisses, unwrapped**

1. Preheat oven to 350°F. Crumble cookie dough into **Classic Batter Bowl**. Stir in peanut butter until completely blended.

2. Fill **Cookie Press** with dough. Fit press with disk #4, #5 or #1, making sure the number on the disk is facing outward, away from the dough. Press dough onto flat **Baking Stone**, 1 inch apart.

3. Bake 10-12 minutes or until light golden brown. Remove from oven and immediately place a candy kiss in the center of each cookie, pressing down firmly. Cool 1-2 minutes on Baking Stone or until chocolate softens but does not melt. Remove cookies to **Nonstick Cooling Rack**. Cool completely. Repeat with remaining dough. Store cookies in tightly covered container.

Yield: 3 1/2 dozen cookies

Nutrients per serving (1 cookie): Calories 90, Total Fat 4.5 g, Saturated Fat 1.5 g, Cholesterol less than 5 mg, Carbohydrate 10 g, Protein 1 g, Sodium 60 mg, Fiber 0 g
Diabetic exchanges per serving (1 cookie): 1 Starch, 1 Fat (1 Carb, 1 Fat)

# Orangesicle Fruit Ring

*Celebrate a summer day with this refreshingly light vanilla ice cream and orange sherbet dessert ring served with the season's juiciest fresh fruits.*

1 **container (1/2 gallon) fat-free, no sugar added vanilla ice cream**
1 **container (1 quart) orange sherbet**
3 **cups honeydew melon balls**
3 **cups cantaloupe cubes**
2 **kiwi, peeled and sliced**
1 **cup blueberries**
1/2 **pint raspberries**

1. Fit collar of **Springform Pan** around fluted ring base. Place pan in freezer and ice cream (but not sherbet) in refrigerator for 20 minutes. Meanwhile, cut two pieces of **Parchment Paper**, 30 x 2½ inches and 13 x 2½ inches. Brush pan with vegetable oil using **Pastry Brush**. Place paper around inside of collar and around ring in center, brushing ends with oil to seal.

2. Remove sherbet from container and cut into 1-inch-thick slices on **Cutting Board**. Arrange slices in bottom of pan, cutting pieces to make an even layer. Smooth surface with **All-Purpose Spreader**. Repeat with ice cream to fill pan. Smooth surface, cover and freeze until firm, at least 4 hours.

3. When ready to serve, scoop honeydew melon into balls using **Small Scoop**. Cut peeled cantaloupe into cubes using **Crinkle Cutter**. Slice peeled kiwi using **Egg Slicer Plus®**.

4. Place Springform Pan in refrigerator for 10 minutes. Invert onto **Chillzanne® Platter**. Release collar and remove paper around outside of ring. Dip clean kitchen towel in hot water, wring dry and place over base of pan for several minutes until loosened. (Rewarming towel may be necessary.) Remove base and paper around inside of ring. Arrange fruit inside and around frozen ring. Using **Nylon Knife** dipped in hot water, slice ring and serve with fruit using **Large Serving Tongs**.

Yield: 24 servings

LOW FAT Nutrients per serving: Calories 120, Total Fat 1 g, Saturated Fat .5 g, Cholesterol 0 mg, Carbohydrate 28 g, Protein 3 g, Sodium 65 mg, Fiber less than 1 g
Diabetic exchanges per serving: 1 Starch, 1 Fruit (2 Carb)

## Kitchen Tips

**Prep time: 40 minutes**
**Freeze time: 4 hours**
**Stand time: 10 minutes**

### Cook's Tip

▲ Place the **Chillzanne® Platter** in the freezer at the same time as the ice cream ring. When you're ready to serve dessert, it will be ready to keep the ice cream ring and fresh fruit icy cold.

### Tool Tips

▲ Use the **Kitchen Shears** to easily cut away the containers from the sherbet and ice cream.

▲ The **Crinkle Cutter** is a handy tool to cut blocks of sherbet and ice cream into thick slices.

▲ Use the **Nylon Knife** when cutting on the Chillzanne® Platter so as not to scratch the surface.

### Cook's Tips

▲ Accompany warm *Apple Bundles* with scoops of fat-free vanilla frozen yogurt for a low-calorie, low-fat dessert choice.

▲ **Pantry Korintje Cinnamon** is a premium quality Indonesian cinnamon. Combine it with granulated sugar in the **Flour/Sugar Shaker** then sprinkle over cookies, pies and French toast.

### Tool Tip

▲ When cleaning Stoneware pieces like the **Deep Dish Baker**, always let them cool to room temperature first. Use clear, hot water (never any soap or detergent) and the **Nylon Pan Scraper** that comes with each Stoneware piece or the **Easy Clean™ Kitchen Brush**. Rinse and dry Stoneware thoroughly before storing. Stoneware should never be washed in an automatic dishwasher.

# Apple Bundles

*These plump, sweet baked bundles of apple
are de-light-fully delicious.*

2   medium Granny Smith apples
1   package (11 ounces) refrigerated
   bread sticks
1   medium orange
1   tablespoon butter or margarine,
   melted
½   cup sugar
½   teaspoon Pantry Korintje
   Cinnamon

1. Preheat oven to 375°F. Peel, core and slice apples with **Apple Peeler/Corer/Slicer**; cut apples in half crosswise.

2. Unroll dough; separate at perforations to form 12 strips. Place 3-4 apple slices at the end of each strip of dough and roll up. Arrange bundles in **Deep Dish Baker**.

3. Zest orange to measure 1 teaspoon zest using **Lemon Zester/Scorer**; set aside. Juice orange to measure ⅓ cup juice; pour juice into bottom of Baker, but not over bundles. Brush melted butter over bundles.

4. Mix zest, sugar and Cinnamon; sprinkle over bundles. Bake 25-30 minutes or until golden brown.

Yield: 12 servings

LOW FAT   Nutrients per serving: Calories 130, Total Fat 2.5 g, Saturated Fat .5 g, Cholesterol less than 5 mg, Carbohydrate 25 g, Protein 2 g, Sodium 200 mg, Fiber less than 1 g
Diabetic exchanges per serving: 1 Starch, ½ Fruit (1½ Carb)

## Kitchen Tips

**Prep time:** 15 minutes
**Bake time:** 12-15 minutes
**Cool time:** 30 minutes

### Cook's Tip

▲ To garnish dessert, microwave 2 squares (1 ounce each) semi-sweet chocolate for baking with 2 teaspoons vegetable oil on HIGH 1 minute, stirring after 30 seconds. Stir until smooth. Place chocolate mixture in small, resealable plastic bag. Cut small tip from corner. Drizzle chocolate over plate. Add drops of chocolate to edge of plate, if desired. Place wedge of dessert over chocolate drizzle. Garnish with fresh strawberry fan (see Tool Tip, p. 86).

### Tool Tip

▲ Chop the nuts in the cap of your **Food Chopper**. It's a great chopping surface for small amounts of food.

# Chocolate Chip Sensation

*This decadent dessert pizza has been a*
*Kitchen Show favorite for years.*

1 package (18 ounces) refrigerated chocolate chip cookie dough
1 package (8 ounces) cream cheese, softened
1/3 cup sugar
1 pint (2 cups) cold half-and-half
1 package (3.9 ounces) chocolate instant pudding and pie filling
1/4 cup chopped nuts

1. Preheat oven to 350°F. Shape cookie dough into a ball in center of **Large Round Stone**. Using lightly floured **Baker's Roller™**, roll out dough to 12-inch circle, about 1/4 inch thick. Bake 12-15 minutes or until edge is set. (Cookie will be soft. Do not overbake.) Cool 10 minutes. Carefully loosen cookie from Baking Stone using **Serrated Bread Knife**; cool completely on Baking Stone.

2. In **Small Batter Bowl**, mix cream cheese and sugar until well blended; set aside. Pour half-and-half into **Classic Batter Bowl**; add pudding mix and whisk 2 minutes using **Stainless Steel Whisk**. Let stand 5 minutes until thickened.

3. Spread cream cheese mixture over thoroughly cooled cookie to within 1/2 inch of edge using **Large Spreader**. Spread pudding over cream cheese. Sprinkle with nuts. Cut into wedges using **Slice 'N Serve®**. Serve immediately or refrigerate.

Yield: 16 servings

Nutrients per serving: Calories 290, Total Fat 16 g, Saturated Fat 8 g, Cholesterol 35 mg, Carbohydrate 31 g, Protein 3 g, Sodium 260 mg, Fiber less than 1 g
Diabetic exchanges per serving: 1 Starch, 3 Fat (2 Carb, 3 Fat)

# Easy Melon Ice

*Create a frosty melon ice with just three ingredients.*
*Watermelon, cantaloupe and honeydew melon are equally refreshing.*

6   cups cubed watermelon
    (4½ pounds with rind)
1   lemon
½   cup sugar
    Edible flowers (optional)

1. Carefully cut watermelon away from rind; cut into 1-inch cubes. On **Large Grooved Cutting Board**, finely chop melon using **Food Chopper**. Place melon and any juice in **Classic Batter Bowl**.

2. Juice lemon to measure 3 tablespoons juice. Add lemon juice and sugar to watermelon; mix well.

3. Divide fruit mixture evenly among 3 **Ice Shaver Tubs**; freeze until firm. Remove frozen mixture from tubs; shave using **Ice Shaver**. Garnish with edible flowers, if desired.

Yield: 8 servings

LOW FAT   Nutrients per serving: Calories 90, Total Fat 0 g, Saturated Fat 0 g, Cholesterol 0 mg, Carbohydrate 21 g, Protein less than 1 g, Sodium 0 mg, Fiber 0 g
Diabetic exchanges per serving: 1½ Fruit (1½ Carb)

# Easy Melon Slush

*Serve this icy drink in a tall, frosted glass garnished with a mint leaf.*

2   tubs frozen *Easy Melon Ice* (see above)
1   liter (4 cups) chilled ginger ale carbonated soda

1. Remove frozen mixture from tubs; shave using **Ice Shaver**.

2. Place shaved ice and carbonated soda in **Quick-Stir® Pitcher**; plunge to mix. Pour into chilled glasses and serve immediately.

Yield: 8 servings

LOW FAT   Nutrients per serving: Calories 100, Total Fat 0 g, Saturated Fat 0 g, Cholesterol 0 mg, Carbohydrate 26 g, Protein 0 g, Sodium 10 mg, Fiber 0 g
Diabetic exchanges per serving: 2 Fruit (2 Carb)

## Kitchen Tips

**Prep time:** 15 minutes
**Freeze time:** 6 hours or overnight

### Cook's Tips

▲ If using cantaloupe, substitute cantaloupe melon (approximately 3 pounds with rind) for the watermelon and orange juice for the lemon juice.

▲ If using honeydew, substitute honeydew melon (approximately 3½ pounds with rind) for the watermelon and lime juice for the lemon juice.

▲ To easily remove the frozen ice mixtures from the plastic tubs, line tubs with plastic wrap before filling.

### Tool Tip

▲ Place the **Chillzanne® Mini-Bowl** in the freezer at the same time that you freeze the melon mixture. It will keep the shaved ice frosty for serving and can be used to store any leftovers.

# Apple Crisp Cake

*Serve up squares of this cinnamon-spiced apple cake tonight, then enjoy the leftovers for breakfast tomorrow morning.*

1 package (17.4 ounces) cinnamon swirl quick bread & coffee cake mix, divided
1/2 cup water
2 eggs
4 tablespoons butter or margarine, melted, divided
4 medium Granny Smith apples (about 1½ pounds)
1/2 cup old-fashioned or quick oats
1/2 teaspoon Pantry Korintje Cinnamon
Caramel ice cream topping and thawed, frozen whipped topping (optional)

1. Preheat oven to 350°F. Spray **Square Baker** with nonstick cooking spray. Remove 1/4 cup of the quick bread mix from large packet; set aside for streusel topping. Combine remaining quick bread mix, water and eggs in **Classic Batter Bowl**. Place butter in **Small Micro-Cooker®**. Microwave on HIGH 45-60 seconds or until melted. Add 2 tablespoons of the melted butter to cake ingredients in Batter Bowl. Stir 50-75 strokes until well blended. Spread into Baker.

2. Peel, core and slice apples using **Apple Peeler/Corer/Slicer**. Cut apple slices into eighths. Arrange apples evenly over batter.

3. Combine small packet of swirl mix, oats, 1/4 cup reserved quick bread mix, remaining 2 tablespoons melted butter and Cinnamon in **Small Batter Bowl**; mix well. Sprinkle mixture evenly over apples.

4. Bake 40-45 minutes or until **Cake Tester** inserted in center comes out clean. Serve warm or at room temperature. Drizzle with ice cream topping and top with whipped topping, if desired.

Yield: 12 servings

Nutrients per serving: Calories 260, Total Fat 10 g, Saturated Fat 4 g, Cholesterol 45 mg, Carbohydrate 40 g, Protein 3 g, Sodium 210 mg, Fiber 1 g
Diabetic exchanges per serving: 1 Starch, 1½ Fruit, 2 Fat (2½ Carb, 1½ Fat)

## Kitchen Tips

**Prep time:** 20 minutes
**Bake time:** 40-45 minutes
**Cool time:** 1 hour

### Cook's Tips

▲ Ground cinnamon can be substituted for Korintje Cinnamon, if desired.

▲ If using a cake mix that includes a packet of glaze, drizzle glaze over cake just before serving.

### Tool Tip

▲ Use the **Apple Wedger** to cut peeled, cored and sliced apples into small wedges to sprinkle over cake batter. The Apple Wedger comes in handy when packing brown bag lunches, too. Wedge your apple, but don't break through the skin at the bottom. Lift up the Wedger to remove, then wrap the whole apple in plastic wrap. The apple will be sectioned, but won't turn brown.

Prep time: 30 minutes
Bake time: 15-18 minutes
Cool time: 45 minutes

### Cook's Tip

▲ It's important to bake the brownie crust on **Parchment Paper**. Otherwise, the batter will run off the **Large Round Stone** during baking.

### Tool Tips

▲ Slice the bananas with our **Egg Slicer Plus®**. It's also great for slicing strawberries and kiwi fruit!

▲ Pour melted chocolate into the blade of the **V-Shaped Cutter**, then drizzle chocolate over pizza.

# Peanutty Brownie Pizza

*Use a packaged mix to make the fudgy brownie crust for this simply irresistible dessert pizza.*

1 package (19-21 ounces) fudge brownie mix (plus ingredients to make brownies)
1 package (8 ounces) cream cheese, softened
1/2 cup packed brown sugar
1/4 cup creamy peanut butter
2 packages (1.6 ounces each) peanut butter cup candy, chopped
1/4 cup peanuts, chopped
2 bananas, sliced
2 tablespoons (1 ounce) semi-sweet chocolate morsels
1 teaspoon vegetable oil

1. Preheat oven to 375°F. Cut a circle of **Parchment Paper** to fit **Large Round Stone**; place on Baking Stone. Prepare brownie mix according to package directions in **Classic Batter Bowl**. Pour brownie batter onto parchment, spreading evenly into a 13-inch circle. Bake 15-18 minutes or until brownie is set. (Do not overbake.) Cool completely.

2. Mix cream cheese, brown sugar and peanut butter until smooth. Using **Large Spreader**, spread cream cheese mixture over brownie to within 1/2 inch of edge.

3. Chop candy and peanuts using **Food Chopper**; sprinkle over cream cheese mixture. Arrange bananas over brownie.

4. Microwave chocolate with oil, uncovered, on HIGH 1 1/2 minutes or until chocolate is melted, stirring after 1 minute. Drizzle over pizza. Cut into squares with **Pizza Cutter**. Serve using **Mini-Serving Spatula**.

Yield: 16 servings

Nutrients per serving: Calories 390, Total Fat 22 g, Saturated Fat 6 g, Cholesterol 40 mg, Carbohydrate 43 g, Protein 6 g, Sodium 210 mg, Fiber 1 g
Diabetic exchanges per serving: 2 Starch, 1 Fruit, 4 Fat (3 Carb, 4 Fat)

# Cool Cookie-wiches

*Mix and match pudding flavors, crackers, cookies and decorations
for endless variations of this frozen snack.*

1½  cups cold milk
  1  package (3.4-3.9 ounces) banana,
     chocolate or vanilla instant pudding
     and pie filling
  2  cups thawed, frozen whipped
     topping
 20  graham cracker squares or 3-inch
     round cookies
     **Optional decorations: sprinkles,
     decors, chopped nuts, miniature
     semi-sweet chocolate morsels or
     miniature candy-coated chocolate
     pieces**

1. Pour milk into **Classic Batter Bowl**; add
   pudding mix and whisk 2 minutes or
   until pudding begins to thicken using
   **Stainless Steel Whisk**. Fold in whipped
   topping.

2. Place lid on bottom of **Bread Tube**; fill
   tube with pudding mixture. Place lid on
   top. Freeze until firm, 4 hours or
   overnight.

3. To unmold, wrap a warm, damp kitchen
   towel around tube 1-2 minutes to loosen
   frozen mixture. Remove caps from tube
   and push mixture out onto **Cutting
   Board**. Cut frozen mixture crosswise into
   10 equal slices.

4. For each cookie-wich, place frozen
   pudding slice between 2 graham cracker
   squares or cookies. Roll edges of cookie-
   wiches in decorations, if desired. Serve
   immediately or wrap individually in
   aluminum foil. Store in freezer.

Yield: 10 sandwich cookies

Nutrients per serving (1 sandwich cookie): Calories 150,
Total Fat 4.5 g, Saturated Fat 3 g, Cholesterol less than 5 mg,
Protein 2 g, Sodium 240 mg, Fiber less than 1 g
Diabetic exchanges per serving (1 sandwich cookie): 1
Starch, ½ Fruit, ½ Fat (1½ Carb, ½ Fat)

*Variations:* **Grasshopper Cookie-wiches:**
Prepare pudding mixture as directed using
1 package (3.3 ounces) white chocolate
instant pudding and pie filling, ¼ teaspoon
peppermint extract and a drop of green food
coloring. Place frozen pudding slices
between chocolate graham cracker squares.
Roll edges in miniature semi-sweet chocolate
morsels.

**Peanut Butter Cookie-wiches:** Use vanilla
instant pudding and pie filling. Add ¼ cup
peanut butter with pudding mix to milk.
Prepare as directed. Place frozen pudding
slices between chocolate graham cracker
squares. Roll edges in chopped peanuts.

**Slim 'n Cool Cookie-wiches:** Use fat-free
milk, sugar-free pudding and pie filling,
frozen fat-free whipped topping and
reduced-fat graham crackers. Prepare as
directed.

LOW FAT  Nutrients per serving (1 sandwich
cookie): Calories 100, Total Fat 1 g,
Saturated Fat 0 g, Cholesterol 0 mg, Carbohydrate 20 g,
Protein 3 g, Sodium 150 mg, Fiber less than 1 g
Diabetic exchanges per serving (1 sandwich cookie): 1 Starch
(1 Carb)

## Kitchen Tips

**Prep time: 10 minutes**
**Freeze time: 4 hours**

### Cook's Tips

▲ To get a variety of
cookies without
purchasing several
packages, look for
cookies in the bulk
food section of your
grocery store.

▲ Cinnamon and
chocolate graham
crackers are also good
choices for this frozen
treat.

### Tool Tip

▲ Either shape **Bread
Tube** can be used for
these *Cool Cookie-
wiches,* but we like
using the square
shape with graham
cracker squares and
the scalloped shape
with round cookies.

# Angel Almond Macaroons

*Just four ingredients (plus water) go into these chewy cookies chock-full of sweet coconut. Serve with a scoop of refreshing Strawberry Ice.*

3/4 cup slivered almonds, coarsely chopped

1 package (16 ounces) angel food cake mix

1/2 cup cold water

1 teaspoon almond extract

1 package (14 ounces) sweetened flaked coconut

1/2 cup miniature semi-sweet chocolate morsels (optional)

1. Preheat oven to 325°F. Cut a rectangle of **Parchment Paper** to cover **Rectangle Stone**. Coarsely chop almonds using **Food Chopper**; set aside.

2. In **Classic Batter Bowl**, stir cake mix, water and almond extract just until moistened. Add half of the coconut, mixing just until blended. Add remaining coconut, mixing just until blended. Stir in chocolate morsels, if desired.

3. Using **Small Scoop**, drop level scoops of coconut mixture, 2 inches apart, onto parchment. Press almonds into tops. Bake 20-24 minutes or until tops are golden. Cool 2 minutes on Baking Stone; remove cookies to **Nonstick Cooling Rack**. Cool completely. Repeat with remaining coconut mixture. Store cookies in tightly covered container.

Yield: 4 dozen cookies

Nutrients per serving (1 cookie): Calories 90, Total Fat 4 g, Saturated Fat 2.5 g, Cholesterol 0 mg, Carbohydrate 12 g, Protein 2 g, Sodium 90 mg, Fiber less than 1 g
Diabetic exchanges per serving (1 cookie): 1 Starch, 1 Fat (1 Carb, 1 Fat)

# Strawberry Ice

1 package (16 ounces) frozen strawberries in sugar, thawed and mashed

1 can (12 ounces) frozen apple juice concentrate, thawed

1 teaspoon lime zest

2 tablespoons lime juice

1/2 cup water

1. Place strawberries in **Classic Batter Bowl**; mash with **Nylon Masher**. Add remaining ingredients; mix well.

2. Divide mixture evenly among 3 **Ice Shaver Tubs**; freeze until firm. Remove frozen mixture from tubs; shave using **Ice Shaver**.

Yield: 8 servings

LOW FAT   Nutrients per serving: Calories 80, Total Fat 0 g, Saturated Fat 0 g, Cholesterol 0 mg, Carbohydrate 20 g, Protein less than 1 g, Sodium 5 mg, Dietary Fiber 1 g
Diabetic exchanges per serving: 1 Starch (1 Carb)

## Kitchen Tips

**Prep time:** 15 minutes
**Bake time:** 20-24 minutes per batch
**Cool time:** 15 minutes

### Tool Tips

▲ Using **Parchment Paper** will prevent cookies from sticking to the **Rectangle Stone** and make cleanup a breeze. You can use the same piece of parchment to bake each batch of cookies, or if you like, scoop all of the coconut mixture at once onto three separate sheets then transfer each sheet to the Baking Stone when ready to bake.

▲ A Pampered Chef **Bamboo Spoon** is the perfect tool for mixing up this heavy cookie dough. Bamboo is a stronger material than what is used for many other wooden spoons, and it resists staining and warping.

Prep time: 15 minutes
Bake time: 18-20 minutes
Cool time: 30 minutes
Chill time: 1 hour

### Cook's Tip

▲ Bite-size, reduced-fat chocolate chip cookies can be substituted for the double chocolate chip cookies.

### Tool Tips

▲ You'll find the **Deluxe Mini-Muffin Pan** is helpful in preparing all kinds of party foods, both sweet and savory. Kids, especially, love bite-size muffins, and the pan's miniature cups make perfect molds for ever-popular gelatin snacks.

▲ The **Small Scoop** is a practical tool for filling tart shells, scooping cookie doughs, making melon balls and forming meatballs.

# Petite Chocolate Cherry Cheesecakes

*Maraschino cherries give these dainty cheesecakes their pretty pink color.*
*Miniature cookies form the crusts.*

| | |
|---|---|
| 24 | bite-size, reduced-fat double chocolate chip cookies |
| 1 | package (8 ounces) reduced-fat cream cheese (Neufchâtel) |
| ¼ | cup sugar |
| ¼ | teaspoon vanilla |
| 1 | egg |
| ¼ | cup reduced-fat sour cream |
| ¼ | cup maraschino cherries (about 14 cherries), well drained, finely chopped |
| 2 | tablespoons miniature semi-sweet chocolate morsels |

1. Preheat oven to 325°F. Place paper liners in cups of **Deluxe Mini-Muffin Pan**. Place one cookie in each liner.

2. In **Small Batter Bowl**, mix cream cheese, sugar and vanilla until well blended. Add egg; mix well. Stir in sour cream.

3. Drain cherries on paper towels. Chop finely with **Chef's Knife** and drain again on paper towels before stirring into batter. Using **Small Scoop**, top each cookie with rounded scoop of batter; spread evenly. Sprinkle evenly with chocolate morsels.

4. Bake 18-20 minutes or until filling is almost set. Cool completely in pan. Remove cheesecakes from pan and refrigerate 1 hour or overnight.

Yield: 24 mini cheesecakes

LOW FAT   Nutrients per serving (1 mini cheesecake): Calories 60, Total Fat 3 g, Saturated Fat 2 g, Cholesterol 20 mg, Carbohydrate 6 g, Protein 1 g, Sodium 60 mg, Fiber 0 g
Diabetic exchanges per serving (1 mini cheesecake): ½ Starch, ½ Fat (½ Carb, ½ Fat)

Prep time: 25 minutes
Bake time: 14-15 minutes
Cool time: 15 minutes

### Cook's Tip

▲ When cutting pie crusts into wedges, a ruler can be used as a guide for the **Pizza Cutter.**

### Tool Tips

▲ Spoon glaze into the blade of the **V-Shaped Cutter** and drizzle over pastries.

▲ There are three flat **Baking Stones** available from the Pampered Chef. The **Classic Round Stone** is 13 inches in diameter, the **Large Round Stone** is 15 inches in diameter and the **Rectangle Stone** measures 12 x 15 inches. The benefits to baking with Stoneware are numerous. Because Stoneware heats evenly and then retains that heat, it produces exceptionally crisp crusts and moist interiors and promotes even baking and browning.

# Nutty Crescent Pastries

*A simple filling of rich milk chocolate, chopped nuts and cinnamon gets rolled in triangles of convenience pastry for these tempting crescents.*

**Pastries**

- 1 package (15 ounces) refrigerated pie crusts (2 crusts)
- 1/3 cup nuts, finely chopped, divided
- 3 bars (1.55 ounces each) milk chocolate candy
- 1/4 cup granulated sugar
- 3/4 teaspoon Pantry Korintje Cinnamon

**Glaze**

- 1/2 cup powdered sugar
- 2 teaspoons milk

1. Preheat oven to 425°F. For pastries, let pie crusts stand at room temperature 15 minutes. Finely chop nuts using **Food Chopper.** Break chocolate into squares and place in **Small Micro-Cooker®.** Microwave, uncovered, on HIGH 1 minute, or until chocolate is melted and smooth, stirring after 30 seconds. Stir in 3 tablespoons of the nuts, sugar and Cinnamon; set aside.

2. Cut each crust into 16 wedges using **Pizza Cutter.** Place a rounded 1/2 teaspoon of the chocolate mixture onto widest end of each wedge. Starting at widest end of wedge, roll up to opposite point. Place point side down on flat **Baking Stone.**

3. Bake 14-15 minutes or until light golden brown. Remove pastries to **Nonstick Cooling Rack**; cool completely.

4. For glaze, mix powdered sugar and milk until smooth; drizzle over cooled pastries. Sprinkle evenly with remaining nuts.

Yield: 32 pastries

Nutrients per serving (1 pastry): Calories 100, Total Fat 5 g, Saturated Fat 2.5 g, Cholesterol less than 5 mg, Carbohydrate 12 g, Protein less than 1 g, Sodium 50 mg, Fiber 0 g
Diabetic exchanges per serving (1 pastry): 1 Fruit, 1 Fat (1 Carb, 1 Fat)

# Dessert Classics

*Traditional Favorites with Timeless Appeal*

*Peach Skillet Cobbler p. 36*

**Prep time:** 35 minutes
**Bake time:** 35-40 minutes
**Cool time:** 30 minutes

### Cook's Tips

▲ To peel fresh peaches, bring water to a boil in **Small (2-qt.) Saucepan.** Carefully add peaches using **Nylon Slotted Server.** Remove peaches after 1 minute and plunge into a bowl of cold water. Pull off skins using **Paring Knife.**

▲ Four cans (15 ounces each) sliced peaches in light syrup, drained, can be substituted for fresh peaches. Reduce cornstarch to 1 tablespoon and prepare as recipe directs.

### Tool Tip

▲ Ginger root (fresh ginger) is available in the produce section of most supermarkets. Peel the outer brown skin with a paring knife or vegetable peeler then finely chop with the **Food Chopper.**

# Peach Skillet Cobbler

*Pictured on p. 34*

*Cobbler is named for its biscuit topping, one that resembles cobblestones. Our homespun peach cobbler, with juicy fresh peaches, bakes right in a skillet.*

### Fruit Filling

|       |                                                        |
|-------|--------------------------------------------------------|
| 1/3   | cup sugar                                              |
| 2     | tablespoons cornstarch                                 |
| 1     | teaspoon peeled and finely chopped fresh ginger root   |
| 8     | cups sliced, peeled fresh peaches (about 8 large or 3¾ pounds) |

### Cobbler Topping

|       |                                              |
|-------|----------------------------------------------|
| 1     | cup all-purpose flour                        |
| 1/3   | cup plus 2 teaspoons sugar, divided          |
| 1½    | teaspoons baking powder                      |
| 1/2   | teaspoon salt                                |
| 3     | tablespoons butter or margarine              |
| 1/4   | cup cold water                               |
| 1/4   | teaspoon ground cinnamon                     |
| 1/4   | cup natural sliced almonds                   |
|       | Ice cream or thawed, frozen whipped topping (optional) |
|       | Fresh mint leaves (optional)                 |

1. Preheat oven to 375°F. For fruit filling, mix sugar, cornstarch and ginger in **Small Batter Bowl**; set aside. Slice peaches into ½-inch slices using **Paring Knife.**

2. Toss peaches with cornstarch mixture in large **Colander Bowl** until evenly coated. Spoon into **Large (10-inch) Skillet**; cover with lid. Heat peach mixture over medium heat until mixture begins to bubble.

3. Meanwhile, for cobbler topping, combine flour, 1/3 cup of the sugar, baking powder and salt in **Classic Batter Bowl**. Using **Pastry Blender**, cut in butter until mixture resembles coarse crumbs. Add water; stir just until dough clings together.

4. Remove cover from skillet. Using **Large Scoop**, drop 6 scant scoops of dough, 2 inches apart, over hot filling. (Filling must be very hot so that biscuit dough will bake through. Biscuits will spread during baking.) Combine remaining 2 teaspoons sugar and cinnamon in **Flour/Sugar Shaker**. Sprinkle dough with almonds and sugar-cinnamon mixture.

5. Bake, uncovered, 35-40 minutes or until topping is golden brown. Using **Oven Mitts**, carefully remove skillet to **Nonstick Cooling Rack**. Cool at least 30 minutes before serving. Serve warm with ice cream or whipped topping and garnish with mint leaves, if desired.

Yield: 6 servings

Nutrients per serving: Calories 340, Total Fat 8 g, Saturated Fat 4 g, Cholesterol 15 mg, Carbohydrate 68 g, Protein 4 g, Sodium 370 mg, Fiber 5 g
Diabetic exchanges per serving: 1 Starch, 3½ Fruit, 1 Fat (4½ Carb, 1 Fat)

# Oatmeal Chocolate Raisin Cookies

*Pictured on p. 39*

*Moms get voted #1 when they fill the cookie jar with homemade treats like these.*

1½ cups all-purpose flour
1 teaspoon baking soda
1 teaspoon Pantry Cinnamon Plus™ Spice Blend
1 cup butter or margarine, softened
¾ cup packed brown sugar
½ cup granulated sugar
2 eggs
2¾ cups old-fashioned or quick oats
1½ cups chocolate covered raisins
1 cup chopped pecans (optional)

1. Preheat oven to 350°F. In **Small Batter Bowl**, combine flour, baking soda and Spice Blend; mix well and set aside.

2. In **Classic Batter Bowl**, beat butter and sugars until creamy. Add eggs and beat well. Add flour mixture; mix well. Stir in oats, raisins and pecans, if desired.

3. Using **Medium Scoop**, drop level scoops of dough, 2 inches apart, onto **Rectangle Stone**. Flatten dough slightly.

4. Bake 13-15 minutes or until edges are golden brown. Cool 3-5 minutes on Baking Stone; remove to **Nonstick Cooling Rack**. Cool completely. Repeat with remaining dough. Store cookies in tightly covered container.

Yield: About 3½ dozen cookies

Nutrients per serving (1 cookie): Calories 130, Total Fat 6 g, Saturated Fat 3.5 g, Cholesterol 20 mg, Carbohydrate 18 g, Protein 2 g, Sodium 80 mg, Fiber less than 1 g.
Diabetic exchanges per serving (1 cookie): 1 Starch, 1 Fat (1 Carb, 1 Fat)

## Kitchen Tips

**Prep time: 20 minutes**
**Bake time: 13-15 minutes per batch**
**Cool time: 20 minutes**

### Cook's Tips

▲ You can substitute pumpkin pie spice or ground cinnamon for the Spice Blend, if you like.

▲ If you prefer, substitute dark or golden raisins for the chocolate covered variety and walnuts for pecans.

### Tool Tip

▲ Use the **Mix 'N Scraper®** to stir the oats, raisins and nuts into the cookie dough. It's a spoon and spatula all in one… just the perfect tool for mixing ingredients into heavy doughs.

## Kitchen Tips

**Prep time:** 15 minutes
**Bake time:** 30-40 minutes
**Cool time:** 1 hour

### Cook's Tips

▲ Use only butter, never margarine or vegetable oil spread, for these rich, tender cookies.

▲ Adding cornstarch along with the flour gives this shortbread a light, delicate texture.

▲ Toasting the pecans makes them more flavorful and adds crunch. Try toasting nuts for other cookies, too. You'll notice a tasty difference.

# Brown Sugar Shortbread

*Scottish in origin, shortbread gets its name from the fact that the dough is so "short" or rich in butter.*

| | |
|---|---|
| 1 | cup pecan halves, chopped, toasted and divided |
| 2¼ | cups all-purpose flour |
| 2 | tablespoons cornstarch |
| ½ | teaspoon salt |
| 1 | cup butter, softened |
| ½ | cup packed brown sugar |

1. Preheat oven to 350°F. Coarsely chop pecans with **Food Chopper**. Heat **Small Sauté Pan** over medium-high heat until hot. Add pecans; toast 1-2 minutes, stirring frequently until nuts are golden brown. Remove pecans from pan; set aside.

2. In **Small Batter Bowl**, combine flour, cornstarch and salt; mix well. In **Classic Batter Bowl**, beat butter and brown sugar until creamy. Add flour mixture and ½ cup of the toasted pecans; mix well. (Dough will be crumbly.)

3. Turn dough out onto floured **Cutting Board**; knead gently just until dough holds together. Form dough into a ball then flatten into a disk and place on **Classic Round Stone**. Using floured **Baker's Roller™**, roll out dough to a 10-inch circle, about ⅜ inch thick, shaping with fingers if necessary. Sprinkle remaining pecans over dough, pressing nuts into dough.

4. With **Pizza Cutter**, lightly score dough (cut about ⅛ inch deep) into 16 equal wedges. (This will make cutting baked shortbread easier.) Bake 35-40 minutes or until deep golden brown.

5. Cool 10 minutes on Baking Stone. Using Pizza Cutter, cut shortbread into wedges; remove to **Nonstick Cooling Rack**. Cool completely. Store in tightly covered container.

Yield: 16 cookies

Nutrients per serving: Calories 230, Total Fat 16 g, Saturated Fat 8 g, Cholesterol 30 mg, Carbohydrate 22 g, Protein 2 g, Sodium 190 mg, Fiber less than 1 g
Diabetic exchanges per serving: 1 Starch, ½ Fruit, 3 Fat (1½ Carb, 3 Fat)

*Brown Sugar Shortbread,
Oatmeal Chocolate Raisin Cookies p. 37*

Prep time: 30 minutes
Bake time: 55-60 minutes
Cool time: 3-4 hours

## Cook's Tips

▲ Before removing your pie from the oven, check that the fruit filling is bubbling in the center and that the juices look clear. Cloudy juices mean the thickener, in this case the cornstarch, hasn't had enough baking time to do its job and the pie filling will be runny.

▲ Brushing the bottom crust with beaten egg white, before it is filled with the fruit mixture, helps prevent it from becoming soggy.

## Tool Tip

▲ You'll discover several Pampered Chef tools are handy to have when making this pretty pie. Use the **Egg Slicer Plus®** to quickly slice strawberries and the **Lemon Zester/Scorer** to zest fresh lemon peel.

# Triple Berry Cherry Pie

*Come fresh berry season, treat your family to just about the tastiest pie ever created.*

1 **package (15 ounces) refrigerated pie crusts (2 crusts)**
¾ **cup sugar**
⅓ **cup cornstarch**
1½ **cups sliced fresh strawberries (about 8 ounces)**
1 **cup fresh blueberries**
1 **cup fresh raspberries**
1 **teaspoon lemon zest**
1 **tablespoon lemon juice**
1 **egg white, lightly beaten**
1 **can (21 ounces) cherry pie filling**

1. Preheat oven to 375°F. Let pie crusts stand at room temperature 15 minutes. Meanwhile, combine sugar and cornstarch in **Classic Batter Bowl**. Add strawberries, blueberries, raspberries, lemon zest and juice. Mix gently to coat fruit.

2. Gently unfold one pie crust onto lightly floured surface. Roll crust to 11½-inch circle using floured **Baker's Roller™**. Place crust in **Deep Dish Pie Plate**, pressing dough into bottom and up sides. Using **Pastry Brush**, brush pie crust with some of the egg white.

3. Fold cherry pie filling into fruit mixture. Spoon fruit mixture into crust.

4. Place remaining pie crust, folded in half, on **Cutting Board**. Starting at fold, cut crust into 15 strips (¾ inch wide) using **Crinkle Cutter**; discard short strips on ends. Set aside 3 strips from the center. Unfold and twist remaining strips. Lay 5 of the twisted strips evenly across the filling in one direction. Lay 5 remaining twisted strips in the opposite direction, forming a crisscross lattice pattern. Firmly press ends of strips onto top edge of crust. Brush edge with egg white. Unfold reserved strips and place end to end over crust edge, trimming ends to fit, if necessary. Press edge firmly to seal.

5. Cover edge of pie with 2- to 3-inch-wide strips of aluminum foil. Bake 55-60 minutes or until filling is bubbly in center and crust is golden brown. Cool 3-4 hours before serving. Cut into wedges.

Yield: 8 servings

Nutrients per serving: Calories 440, Total Fat 14 g, Saturated Fat 6 g, Cholesterol 10 mg, Carbohydrate 78 g, Protein 3 g, Sodium 10 mg, Fiber 2 g
Diabetic exchanges per serving: 1 Starch, 4 Fruit, 2½ Fat (5 Carb, 2 Fat)

# Quick Carrot Cake

*It's hard to believe this spicy fluted cake starts with a cake mix and "bakes" in the microwave oven.*

2 cups grated carrots (about 3 medium)

3 eggs

1 can (8 ounces) crushed pineapple in juice, undrained

1 tablespoon Pantry Korintje Cinnamon

1 package (18.25 ounces) yellow cake mix

1/3 cup vegetable oil

1/2 cup coarsely chopped walnuts, divided

4 ounces cream cheese, softened

1/2 cup powdered sugar

6-7 teaspoons milk

1. Brush **Stoneware Fluted Pan** with vegetable oil using **Pastry Brush**. Grate carrots with **Ultimate Slice & Grate**; set aside.

2. In **Classic Batter Bowl**, combine eggs, pineapple with juice and Cinnamon. Add cake mix and 1/3 cup oil; mix with **Mix 'N Scraper®** until thoroughly blended, about 1 minute. Fold in carrots and all but 2 tablespoons of the walnuts. Pour batter into pan, spreading evenly.

3. Microwave on HIGH 10-13 minutes or until **Cake Tester** inserted near center comes out clean. (Cake will be slightly moist on top, near center.) Let stand in microwave oven 10 minutes. Loosen cake from sides and center tube of pan, if necessary. Invert onto **Nonstick Cooling Rack**; remove pan. Cool completely.

4. In **Small Batter Bowl**, combine cream cheese, powdered sugar and enough milk to make a thick glaze. Spoon glaze over top of cake. Sprinkle with remaining walnuts. Let cake stand until glaze is set before slicing.

Yield: 12 servings

Nutrients per serving: Calories 360, Total Fat 19 g, Saturated Fat 4 g, Cholesterol 65 mg, Carbohydrate 45 g, Protein 5 g, Sodium 340 mg, Fiber 2 g
Diabetic exchanges per serving: 2 Starch, 1 Fruit, 3 Fat (3 Carb, 3 Fat)

*Variation:* **Banana Walnut Cake:** Omit carrots and pineapple. Combine 1 1/2 cups mashed bananas (about 4 medium) with eggs and Cinnamon before adding cake mix and oil. Prepare as directed except microwave cake on HIGH 10-12 minutes.

## Kitchen Tips

Prep time: 20 minutes
Microwave time: 10-13 minutes
Cool time: 45 minutes

### Cook's Tips

▲ If using a microwave oven without a built-in turn table, rotate cake once after 6 minutes of cooking.

▲ To bake cake in a conventional oven, preheat oven to 325°F. Bake 55-60 minutes or until **Cake Tester** inserted in center comes out clean. Cool 10 minutes. Invert onto cooling rack; remove pan. Cool completely.

▲ Substitute ground cinnamon for Korintje Cinnamon, if desired.

### Tool Tips

▲ For ease in serving, slice cake with our **Serrated Bread Knife**.

▲ The **Citrus Peeler** is the perfect tool to aid in loosening cakes from the fluted sides and center of the **Stoneware Fluted Pan**.

# Banana Split Shortcakes

*With flavors from the ice cream shop,*
*these individual shortcakes are irresistible.*

**Shortcakes**
- 2 cups all-purpose flour
- 1/3 cup sugar
- 1 tablespoon baking powder
- 1/4 teaspoon salt
- 1/3 cup (5 1/3 tablespoons) stick vegetable oil spread (70% fat)
- 2/3 cup fat-free (skim) milk
- 1 egg white, lightly beaten

**Filling**
- 1 cup sliced strawberries
- 1 tablespoon sugar
- 1 can (8 ounces) pineapple tidbits in juice, undrained
- 1 medium banana, sliced
- 1/2 cup chocolate-flavored syrup
- 1 quart fat-free, no sugar added vanilla ice cream
- 1/4 cup chopped almonds (optional)
  Thawed, frozen whipped topping (optional)

1. Preheat oven to 375°F. For shortcakes, combine flour, sugar, baking powder and salt in **Classic Batter Bowl**. Remove 1/4 cup of the flour mixture; set aside. Using **Pastry Blender**, cut in vegetable oil spread just until mixture resembles coarse crumbs. Add milk; stir just until dough clings together. Turn out onto **Cutting Board** sprinkled with some of the reserved flour mixture. Knead gently 8-10 times adding remaining reserved flour mixture.

2. Roll dough to 1/2 inch thickness with lightly floured **Baker's Roller™**. Cut with **Bread Tube** dipped in flour. Gather dough scraps and re-roll dough to make 8 shortcakes. Transfer shortcakes to **Rectangle Stone**. Brush with egg white using **Pastry Brush**.

3. Bake 17-19 minutes or until golden brown. Remove shortcakes to **Nonstick Cooling Rack**. Cool completely.

4. Meanwhile, for filling, gently toss strawberries with sugar in **Small Batter Bowl**; let stand at least 30 minutes. Add pineapple with juice and banana to strawberries in Batter Bowl; mix gently. Split shortcakes in half using **Serrated Bread Knife**.

5. For each serving, spoon 1 tablespoon chocolate syrup on serving plate; top with bottom half of shortcake. Scoop ice cream over bottom half. Spoon fruit mixture over ice cream. Top with nuts and whipped topping, if desired. Cover with top half of shortcake.

Yield: 8 servings

Nutrients per serving: Calories 370, Total Fat 7 g, Saturated Fat 1.5 g, Cholesterol 0 mg, Carbohydrate 71 g, Protein 9 g, Sodium 420 mg, Fiber 2 g
Diabetic exchanges per serving: 3 Starch, 2 Fruit, 1 Fat (5 Carb)

## Kitchen Tips

**Prep time: 40 minutes**
**Bake time: 17-19 minutes**
**Cool time: 20 minutes**

### Cook's Tip

▲ To reduce calories and fat, this recipe calls for a reduced-fat spread that comes in a stick form instead of butter or margarine. We recommend a vegetable oil spread with at least 70% fat.

### Tool Tips

▲ Use the **Egg Separator**, which conveniently fits over the rim of most bowls, to separate the egg. The spiral wire basket can be used to lightly beat the egg white. Cover and refrigerate the yolk to add to scrambled eggs or French toast batter for tomorrow's breakfast.

▲ Strawberries and bananas can be sliced in a jiffy with the **Egg Slicer Plus®**.

# Caramel Pecan Bread Pudding

*The key to a good bread pudding is a dense-textured bread,*
*or in this case, egg bagels.*

**Prep time:** 35 minutes
**Bake time:** 45-50 minutes
**Cool time:** 10 minutes

## Cook's Tips

▲ This old-fashioned dessert comes from the oven puffy and golden brown then falls slowly as it starts to cool. The top is toasted and crunchy while the inside has a soft, spoonable texture.

▲ Substitute ground cinnamon for Korintje Cinnamon, if desired.

## Make-Ahead Tip

▲ This dessert can be assembled several hours in advance. Cover **Oval Baker** with aluminum foil and refrigerate. Remove Baker from the refrigerator 30 minutes before baking. Bake, uncovered, 55-60 minutes.

---

1 package (15 ounces) egg bagels (6 bagels)
3 cups milk
1/4 cup packed brown sugar
3 eggs
1 teaspoon vanilla
1 teaspoon Pantry Korintje Cinnamon
1/2 cup coarsely chopped pecans
1/2 cup butterscotch caramel ice cream topping
   Additional butterscotch caramel ice cream topping (optional)

---

1. Preheat oven to 325°F. With **Serrated Bread Knife**, cut bagels into 1-inch pieces to make 8 cups. Place in **Stoneware Bar Pan**. Bake 15-20 minutes or until lightly toasted. Cool slightly and transfer to **Oval Baker**; set aside.

2. Combine milk, brown sugar, eggs, vanilla and Cinnamon in **Classic Batter Bowl**. Whisk with **Stainless Steel Whisk** until well blended. Pour mixture evenly over bagel pieces. Let stand 15 minutes; mix well.

3. Sprinkle pecans evenly over bagel mixture; drizzle with ice cream topping. Bake 45-50 minutes or until pudding is puffed and knife inserted in center comes out clean. Cool 10 minutes.

4. If desired, microwave additional ice cream topping in **Small Micro-Cooker®** on HIGH 15 seconds or until warm. Spoon pudding into dessert dishes and serve warm with topping.

Yield: 8 servings

Nutrients per serving: Calories 360, Total Fat 18 g, Saturated Fat 3 g, Cholesterol 100 mg, Carbohydrate 55 g, Protein 12 g, Sodium 380 mg, Fiber 2 g
Diabetic exchanges per serving: 3 1/2 Starch, 1 1/2 Fruit, 3 Fat (5 1/2 Carb, 3 Fat)

# Pumpkin Ribbon Cake

*Don't be turned off by the long list of ingredients This cake assembles rather easily and the "from scratch" results are well worth the effort.*

## Cake
- 2½ cups all-purpose flour
- 2 teaspoons baking powder
- 1½ teaspoons Pantry Cinnamon Plus™ Spice Blend
- 1 teaspoon baking soda
- ½ teaspoon salt
- 1½ cups granulated sugar
- ¾ cup butter or margarine, softened
- 3 eggs
- ¾ cup solid pack pumpkin
- ½ cup milk
- 1 teaspoon vanilla

## Filling
- 1 package (8 ounces) cream cheese, softened
- ¼ cup granulated sugar

## Topping
- Powdered sugar
- Thawed, frozen whipped topping (optional)

1. Preheat oven to 350°F. Spray **Deep Dish Baker** with nonstick cooking spray. For cake, combine flour, baking powder, Spice Blend, baking soda and salt in **Small Batter Bowl**; mix well and set aside. In **Classic Batter Bowl**, beat sugar and butter until light and fluffy. Add eggs, pumpkin, milk and vanilla; beat well. Slowly add flour mixture to pumpkin mixture; mix well. Set aside.

2. For filling, whisk cream cheese and granulated sugar until well blended and smooth. Spread 2½ cups of the cake batter evenly over bottom of Baker. Spoon cream cheese mixture evenly over cake batter; carefully spread over batter using **Large Spreader**. Spoon remaining cake batter over cream cheese mixture, spreading evenly.

3. Bake 45-50 minutes or until **Cake Tester** inserted in center comes out clean. Cool completely.

4. Before serving, sprinkle cake with powdered sugar using **Flour/Sugar Shaker**. Cut into wedges using **Slice 'N Serve®**. Serve with whipped topping sprinkled with additional Spice Blend, if desired.

Yield: 12 servings

Nutrients per serving: Calories 400, Total Fat 20 g, Saturated Fat 12 g, Cholesterol 105 mg, Carbohydrate 51 g, Protein 6 g, Sodium 480 mg, Fiber 1 g
Diabetic exchanges per serving: 2 Starch, 1½ Fruit, 3½ Fat (3½ Carb, 3 Fat)

## Kitchen Tips

Prep time: 20 minutes
Bake time: 45-50 minutes
Cool time: 1 hour

### Cook's Tips

▲ Create your own design on top of this cake by making a paper stencil. Using **Parchment Paper**, trace around outer edge of Baker; cut out circle. Fold circle in half, then in half several more times to make a triangle; make cuts along edges to form a pattern. Unfold and place on top of cake. Sprinkle powdered sugar over stencil, then carefully lift stencil from top of cake.

▲ Pumpkin pie spice or ground cinnamon can be substituted for the Cinnamon Plus™ Spice Blend, if desired.

▲ When purchasing pumpkin for this recipe, look for cans containing 100% pumpkin, not a pumpkin pie filling that includes sugar and spices.

Prep time: 25 minutes
Bake time: 50-55 minutes
Cool time: 2 hours

### Cook's Tips

▲ Granny Smith apples are another good choice for this pie. Peel, core and slice the apples if using this variety.

▲ Ground cinnamon can be substituted for the Spice Blend, if desired.

▲ For old-fashioned flavor, substitute raisins for the cranberries.

### Tool Tip

▲ Coarsely chop walnuts using the **Food Chopper**.

# Streusel Apple Cranberry Pie

*Juicy apple slices and crimson cranberries peek through the nutty streusel topping of this homey pie.*

### Streusel Topping

- 1/4 cup all-purpose flour
- 1/4 cup packed brown sugar
- 3 tablespoons butter or margarine
- 1/2 cup coarsely chopped walnuts

### Crust & Fruit Filling

- 1/2 package (15 ounces) refrigerated pie crusts (1 crust)
- 3/4 cup granulated sugar
- 1/4 cup all-purpose flour
- 1 1/4 teaspoons Pantry Cinnamon Plus™ Spice Blend
- 1/4 teaspoon salt
- 1 cup dried cranberries
- 2 teaspoons orange zest
- 7-8 red baking apples, such as Jonathan (about 2 1/2 pounds)

1. Preheat oven to 350°F. For streusel topping, combine flour and brown sugar in **Classic Batter Bowl**. Cut in butter using **Pastry Blender** until mixture is crumbly. Stir in walnuts and set aside.

2. For crust and fruit filling, let pie crust stand at room temperature 15 minutes. Meanwhile, combine sugar, flour, Spice Blend and salt in **Small Batter Bowl**. Add cranberries and orange zest; mix well and set aside.

3. Core and slice apples using **Apple Peeler/Corer/Slicer**. Cut apples in half to make about 8 cups slices. Toss apple slices with sugar mixture in large bowl until evenly coated; set aside.

4. Gently unfold crust onto lightly floured surface. Roll crust to 11 1/2-inch circle using floured **Baker's Roller™**. Place crust into bottom and up sides of **Deep Dish Pie Plate** forming a loose ruffle even with the top edge of the pie plate. Spoon apple mixture into crust. Sprinkle evenly with streusel topping. To prevent over browning of pastry edges, cover edge of pie with 2- to 3-inch-wide strips of aluminum foil.

5. Bake 50-55 minutes or until apples are tender and streusel is golden brown. Cool at least 2 hours before serving. Cut into wedges.

Yield: 8 servings

Nutrients per serving: Calories 410, Total Fat 15 g, Saturated Fat 6 g, Cholesterol 20 mg, Carbohydrate 68 g, Protein 3 g, Sodium 220 mg, Fiber 4 g
Diabetic exchanges per serving: 1 Starch, 3 1/2 Fruit, 3 Fat (4 1/2 Carb, 2 Fat)

# Sweet Potato Pound Cake

*Why not splurge tonight with ice cream, caramel topping and pecans on
a slice of this Southern-style loaf cake?*

**Cake**

| | |
|---|---|
| 1 | package (16 ounces) pound cake mix |
| 1 | jar (6 ounces) strained infant sweet potatoes |
| 2 | eggs |
| 1/3 | cup milk |
| 1 | teaspoon Pantry Cinnamon Plus™ Spice Blend |

**Glaze**

| | |
|---|---|
| 1/2 | cup powdered sugar |
| 3-4 | teaspoons milk |
| 2 | tablespoons pecans, finely grated |

**Toppings**

| | |
|---|---|
| 1 | cup butterscotch caramel ice cream topping |
| 1/4 | teaspoon Pantry Cinnamon Plus™ Spice Blend |
| 3 | cups vanilla ice cream |
| 1/3 | cup chopped pecans |

1. Preheat oven to 350°F. Lightly spray bottom only of **Stoneware Loaf Pan** with nonstick cooking spray. For cake, combine cake mix, sweet potatoes, eggs, milk and Spice Blend in **Classic Batter Bowl**. Mix according to package directions. Pour into pan.

2. Bake 55-60 minutes or until **Cake Tester** inserted in center comes out clean. Cool in pan on **Nonstick Cooling Rack** 15 minutes; loosen edges with knife. Remove from pan; cool completely.

3. For glaze, combine powdered sugar and milk; drizzle over cake. Immediately grate pecans over glaze using **Deluxe Cheese Grater**. Cut cake into slices using **Serrated Bread Knife**.

4. For toppings, microwave ice cream topping in **Small Micro-Cooker®** on HIGH 30-40 seconds or until warm. Stir in Spice Blend. For each serving, top cake slice with ice cream and topping. Sprinkle with pecans.

Yield: 12 servings

Nutrients per serving: Calories 410, Total Fat 26 g, Saturated Fat 6 g, Cholesterol 75 mg, Carbohydrate 60 g, Protein 6 g, Sodium 240 mg, Fiber less than 1 g
Diabetic exchanges per serving: 2 Starch, 2 Fruit, 5 Fat (4 Carb, 4 1/2 Fat)

## Kitchen Tips

Prep time: 20 minutes
Bake time: 55-60 minutes
Cool time: 1 hour

### Cook's Tip

▲ **Pantry Cinnamon Plus™ Spice Blend** is a special blend of Korintje cinnamon, nutmeg, allspice, ground orange peel, cloves and ginger. It's the perfect all-in-one spice blend for baked goods made with sweet potatoes and pumpkin. To substitute our Spice Blend in your favorite recipes, total the amounts of the individual spices, and then use that amount of Cinnamon Plus™.

### Tool Tip

▲ The **Skinny Scraper** is the perfect tool for removing the contents from small jars of baby food.

**Prep time:** 20 minutes
**Bake time:** 60-70 minutes
**Cool time:** 1 hour

### Cook's Tip

▲ Sliced thin and spread with jelly, this fluted cake makes a neat peanut butter and jelly sandwich for after-school snacking.

### Tool Tip

▲ The **Mix 'N Scraper®** is one of three scrapers available from The Pampered Chef. Because it's a large spoon and spatula all in one, it's great for mixing heavy batters and scraping out bowls. The **Classic Scraper** is a traditional size and the scraper you'll turn to most often for general cooking needs. The **Skinny Scraper** is smallest and is the perfect tool for easily removing contents from cans and jars. All three scrapers are heat-safe up to 650°F. and can be used to stir hot foods when cooking in pans or skillets.

# Peanutty Crunch Cake

*The lovely shape of our Stoneware Fluted Pan
lets you turn every cake into one that's really special.*

### Cake

- 2/3 cup all-purpose flour
- 1/3 cup packed brown sugar
- 1/2 cup creamy peanut butter
- 1/3 cup chopped dry roasted peanuts
- 1 package (18.25 ounces) butter recipe yellow cake mix (plus ingredients to make cake)

### Glaze

- 1 cup powdered sugar
- 3-4 teaspoons water
- 1/2 teaspoon vanilla

1. Preheat oven to 325°F. Spray **Stoneware Fluted Pan** with nonstick cooking spray. For cake, combine flour and brown sugar in **Classic Batter Bowl**. Cut in peanut butter with **Pastry Blender** until mixture resembles coarse crumbs; stir in peanuts chopped with **Food Chopper**.

2. Sprinkle half of the peanut butter mixture evenly over bottom of pan. Prepare cake mix according to package directions. Using **Mix 'N Scraper®**, carefully spoon half of the batter over peanut butter mixture in pan; spread evenly. Sprinkle remaining peanut butter mixture over batter in pan; cover with remaining batter.

3. Bake 60-70 minutes or until **Cake Tester** inserted near center comes out clean. Cool in pan 10 minutes. Loosen cake from sides and center tube of pan. Invert onto **Nonstick Cooling Rack**; remove pan. Cool completely.

4. For glaze, combine powdered sugar, water and vanilla; whisk until smooth using **Stainless Steel Whisk**. Drizzle glaze over cake.

Yield: 16 servings

Nutrients per serving: Calories 320, Total Fat 15 g, Saturated Fat 2 g, Cholesterol 40 mg, Carbohydrate 43 g, Protein 6 g, Sodium 280 mg, Fiber 1 g
Diabetic exchanges per serving: 2 Starch, 1 Fruit, 2 1/2 Fat (3 Carb, 2 1/2 Fat)

# Apple-Rhubarb Crisp

*You'll be amazed at the perfect results you get from "baking" this down-home dessert in your microwave oven.*

**Fruit Filling**

- 1 jar (12 ounces) strawberry preserves
- 1/4 cup granulated sugar
- 2 tablespoons all-purpose flour
- 3 medium Granny Smith apples (about 1 pound)
- 3 cups rhubarb, cut into 1/2-inch slices

**Streusel Topping**

- 1/3 cup butter or margarine, melted
- 20 square shortbread cookies (1 1/4 cups chopped)
- 1/2 cup natural whole almonds, chopped
- 1/3 cup all-purpose flour
- 1/4 cup packed brown sugar
- 1/2 teaspoon Pantry Korintje Cinnamon
  Thawed, frozen whipped topping or vanilla ice cream (optional)

1. For fruit filling, mix preserves, sugar and flour in **Small Batter Bowl**; set aside. Peel, core and slice apples using **Apple Peeler/Corer/Slicer**. Cut apples in half crosswise. Combine apple slices and rhubarb in large **Colander Bowl**; add preserves mixture, tossing gently. Spoon filling into **Deep Dish Baker**.

2. For streusel topping, microwave butter in **Large Micro-Cooker®** on HIGH 45-60 seconds or until melted. Chop cookies and almonds using **Food Chopper**. Add cookies, almonds, flour, brown sugar and Cinnamon to melted butter; mix well. Sprinkle mixture evenly over fruit filling.

3. Microwave on HIGH 13-15 minutes or until apples are tender, turning dish after 7 minutes. Let stand about 30 minutes. Serve warm with whipped topping or vanilla ice cream, if desired.

Yield: 8 servings

Nutrients per serving: Calories 420, Total Fat 16 g, Saturated Fat 6 g, Cholesterol 25 mg, Carbohydrate 68 g, Protein 4 g, Sodium 180 mg, Fiber 3 g
Diabetic exchanges per serving: 1 Starch, 3 1/2 Fruit, 3 Fat (4 1/2 Carb, 2 Fat)

***Variation:* Pine-Apple Crisp:** For fruit filling, substitute pineapple preserves for the strawberry preserves. Omit granulated sugar and reduce flour to 1 tablespoon. Omit rhubarb and use 6 medium (2 pounds) peeled, cored and sliced Granny Smith apples. Prepare streusel topping and microwave as recipe directs.

## Kitchen Tips

**Prep time:** 30 minutes
**Microwave time:** 13-15 minutes
**Stand time:** 30 minutes

### Cook's Tips

▲ You'll get excellent results when making these fruit crisps in the microwave oven, but they can be prepared in a conventional oven, too. For fruit fillings, use 3 tablespoons flour in the *Apple-Rhubarb Crisp* and 2 tablespoons flour in the *Pine-Apple Crisp*. Bake at 350°F for 45-50 minutes or until apples are tender.

▲ For a tropical twist to *Pine-Apple Crisp*, substitute crisp coconut bar cookies for the shortbread cookies and ground nutmeg for the Cinnamon.

▲ Ground cinnamon can be substituted for Korintje Cinnamon, if desired.

**Prep time:** 20 minutes
**Bake time:** 30-35 minutes
**Cool time:** 15 minutes

### Tool Tips

▲ All Pampered Chef cookware is oven-safe to 350°F. Although the handles are made of heat-resistant material, they will become hot when cookware is placed in the oven. Be sure to use **Oven Mitts** when removing this cake from the oven.

▲ To avoid scratching interior surfaces, knives or other sharp metal objects shouldn't be used in your Pampered Chef cookware. Special **Nylon Tools** are available to cover almost every cooking need.

# Pineapple Upside-Down Cake

*This moist, tender cake, topped with caramelized pineapple slices, nuts and maraschino cherries, will have everyone asking for more.*

| | |
|---|---|
| 1/2 | cup butter or margarine |
| 1 | cup packed brown sugar |
| 1 | can (20 ounces) pineapple slices, undrained |
| 5 | maraschino cherries, drained and halved |
| 1/2 | cup chopped nuts |
| 1 | package (18.25 ounces) yellow cake mix |
| | Water |
| 3 | eggs |
| 1/3 | cup vegetable oil |
| 1 | cup thawed, frozen whipped topping |

1. Preheat oven to 350°F. Melt butter in **Family (12-inch) Skillet** over low heat. Remove from heat. Stir in brown sugar until well blended using **Nylon Spoon**.

2. Drain pineapple in small **Colander**, reserving juice in small **Colander Bowl**; set aside. Arrange pineapple slices over sugar mixture. Place a cherry half in center of each pineapple slice. Sprinkle nuts over pineapple.

3. Add enough water to pineapple juice to make 1 1/3 cups liquid. Combine cake mix, liquid, eggs and oil in **Classic Batter Bowl**; whisk with **Stainless Steel Whisk** until well blended and smooth. Pour over fruit mixture in skillet.

4. Bake 30-35 minutes or until **Cake Tester** inserted in center comes out clean. Cool 5 minutes. Carefully loosen edge of cake; invert onto large, heat-safe serving plate. Cool slightly. Pipe whipped topping around edge of cake using **Easy Accent® Decorator**. Cut with **Slice 'N Serve®**. Serve warm.

Yield: 12 servings

Nutrients per serving: Calories 470, Total Fat 23 g, Saturated Fat 9 g, Cholesterol 75 mg, Carbohydrate 62 g, Protein 4 g, Sodium 370 mg, Fiber 2 g
Diabetic exchanges per serving: 1 Starch, 3 Fruit, 4 1/2 Fat (4 Carb, 4 Fat)

# Brownie Pudding Cake

*This is the ultimate comfort food dessert – warm, sweet
and oh so chocolatey.*

1¼   cups all-purpose flour
1½   cups granulated sugar, divided
½   cup unsweetened cocoa powder,
        divided
  2   teaspoons baking powder
½   teaspoon salt
¾   cup milk
  3   tablespoons butter or margarine,
        melted
1½   teaspoons vanilla, divided
  1   cup semi-sweet chocolate morsels
1¾   cups boiling water
  1   tablespoon powdered sugar

1. Preheat oven to 350°F. Combine flour,
   ¾ cup of the granulated sugar, ¼ cup of
   the cocoa powder, baking powder and salt
   in **Classic Batter Bowl**. Add milk, melted
   butter and ½ teaspoon of the vanilla; stir
   until smooth. Stir in chocolate morsels.
   Spread batter evenly in **Oval Baker**.

2. In **Small Batter Bowl**, whisk together
   remaining ¾ cup granulated sugar and
   ¼ cup cocoa; gradually stir in boiling
   water and remaining 1 teaspoon vanilla.
   Carefully pour mixture evenly over batter
   in Baker.

3. Bake 30-35 minutes or until **Cake Tester**
   inserted in center comes out clean. Cool
   15 minutes. Sprinkle with powdered sugar
   using **Flour/Sugar Shaker**. Spoon into
   dessert dishes.

Yield: 8 servings

Nutrients per serving: Calories 380, Total Fat 12 g, Saturated
Fat 6 g, Cholesterol 15 mg, Carbohydrate 71g, Protein 4 g,
Sodium 330 mg, Fiber 2 g
Diabetic exchanges per serving: 1 Starch, 4 Fruit, 2 Fat
(5 Carb, 1 Fat)

***Variation:* Brownie Pudding Cake Sundaes**
*(pictured at left):* Top each serving with a
scoop of fudge marble or vanilla ice cream,
chopped peanuts, whipped topping and a
maraschino cherry.

## Kitchen Tips

Prep time: 15 minutes
Bake time: 30-35 minutes
Cool time: 15 minutes

### Cook's Tips

▲ There's a bit of a
mystery going on
here. We can't explain
it, but during the
baking this batter
separates. The cake
rises to the top and
the cocoa pudding
goes to the bottom,
forming a delicious
sauce. Pudding cakes
make wonderful
family desserts and
have been popular
since the 1930s.

▲ Unsweetened cocoa
powder can be found
in the baking aisle of
the supermarket. It's
not the same as cocoa
mixes or instant
cocoa. These products
contain sweeteners
and often dried milk
powder.

# Orange Poppy Seed Tea Bread

*This lovely bread is similar to a pound cake and makes
a delightful dessert, snack or breakfast treat.*

**Tea Bread**

1½ cups all-purpose flour
1 teaspoon baking powder
¼ teaspoon salt
1 tablespoon poppy seeds
2 teaspoons orange zest, finely chopped
½ cup butter or margarine, softened
1 cup granulated sugar
1 teaspoon vanilla
3 eggs
½ cup sour cream

**Glaze**

⅓ cup powdered sugar
2 tablespoons fresh orange juice
1 teaspoon orange zest, finely chopped

1. Preheat oven to 325°F. Spray bottom only of **Stoneware Loaf Pan** with nonstick cooking spray. For tea bread, combine flour, baking powder, salt, poppy seeds and orange zest in **Small Batter Bowl**; mix well and set aside.

2. In **Classic Batter Bowl**, beat butter on high speed of electric mixer 30 seconds. Add sugar; continue beating 3 minutes until mixture is light and fluffy. Add vanilla; beat well.

3. On medium speed, add eggs, one at a time, beating 30 seconds after each. Add one third of the flour mixture, beating on low speed just until combined. Beat in half of the sour cream. Add another one third of the flour mixture, the remaining sour cream, and then the remaining flour mixture, beating after each addition just until combined. Pour batter into pan.

4. Bake 60-65 minutes or until **Cake Tester** inserted in center comes out clean and top is golden brown.

5. Meanwhile, for glaze, combine powdered sugar, orange juice and zest.

6. Immediately remove bread from pan onto **Nonstick Cooling Rack**. Brush some of the glaze onto top and sides of warm bread using **Pastry Brush**. Repeat several times with remaining glaze as bread cools. Cool completely. Cut into slices. To store tea bread, wrap loosely in plastic wrap and store at room temperature.

Yield: 12 servings

Nutrients per serving: Calories 240, Total Fat 11 g, Saturated Fat 6 g, Cholesterol 80 mg, Carbohydrate 33 g, Protein 4 g, Sodium 190 mg, Fiber less than 1 g
Diabetic exchanges per serving: 1 Starch, 1 Fruit, 2 Fat (2 Carb, 2 Fat)

## Kitchen Tips

Prep time: 20 minutes
Bake time: 60-65 minutes
Cool time: 1 hour

### Cook's Tip

▲ Baked goods will have a higher volume when all of the ingredients start at room temperature. For this recipe, remove butter, eggs and sour cream from the refrigerator at least 30 minutes before you begin mixing.

### Tool Tips

▲ One large orange will yield the amount of zest and juice needed for this tea bread. Use the **Lemon Zester/Scorer** to remove long strips of zest (the colored part of the skin), then chop finely with the **Chef's Knife**.

▲ Set your **Clock Timer** for 3 minutes when you begin to beat the butter and sugar. This tender tea bread has a fine texture when the butter and sugar are well beaten.

# Desserts with
# Drama

*Dazzling, Delicious and
Decadent Delights*

Summer Lattice Pastry p. 66

Prep time: 40 minutes
Bake time: 20-25 minutes
Cool time: 10 minutes

### Cook's Tips

▲ Remove pits from plums using **The Corer™**; slice using **Ultimate Slice & Grate.**

▲ To create lattice over top of pastry, attach closed star tip to **Easy Accent® Decorator**; fill with whipped topping. Pipe 3 horizontal rows across fruit, followed by 3 diagonal rows.

### Make-Ahead Tips

▲ Crust and filling can be made up to 1 day in advance; cover and refrigerate.

▲ Fruit can be prepared up to 2 hours in advance. Combine with preserves just before assembling; serve immediately.

# Summer Lattice Pastry

*Pictured on p. 65*
*Serve this pretty French-style pastry for a delightful ending to any summer gathering.*

## Crust
- 1 package (15 ounces) refrigerated pie crusts (2 crusts)
- 1/2 cup sliced almonds, grated, divided
- 1 egg white, lightly beaten

## Filling
- 1 package (3 ounces) vanilla cook and serve pudding and pie filling (not instant)
- 1 cup milk
- 2 tablespoons butter or margarine
- 1/2 teaspoon vanilla

## Toppings
- 4 cups assorted fresh fruit, such as sliced plums and strawberries; blueberries, raspberries or grapes
- 1/4 cup apricot preserves
- 3 cups thawed, frozen whipped topping
- 1/2 teaspoon Pantry Cinnamon Plus™ Spice Blend
  Fresh mint leaves (optional)

1. Preheat oven to 375°F. Let pie crust stand at room temperature 15 minutes. Lightly dust **Large Round Stone** with flour. Unfold one pie crust and place in center of Baking Stone. Lightly brush with water using **Pastry Brush**. Using **Deluxe Cheese Grater**, grate half of the almonds over crust. Unfold second pie crust and place over crust on Baking Stone, matching edges and pressing down to seal. Using **Baker's Roller™**, roll both crusts out together to edge of Baking Stone. Fold 1/2 inch of edge of crust in toward center, forming an even border; press to seal seam. Using smooth end of pastry tool, form a decorative fluted edge. Prick center of crust.

2. Brush edge of crust with egg white using Pastry Brush. Grate remaining almonds evenly over entire crust. Bake 20-25 minutes or until golden brown. Remove to **Nonstick Cooling Rack**. Cool at least 10 minutes.

3. Meanwhile, for filling, combine pudding mix and milk in **Small (2-qt.) Saucepan**; whisk with **Nylon Spiral Whisk**. Cook over medium heat, stirring constantly, until mixture bubbles. Remove from heat. Stir in butter and vanilla; mix until smooth. Cool at least 10 minutes. Using **Large Spreader**, spread filling evenly over crust.

4. Place fruit in **Classic Batter Bowl**. Microwave preserves in **Small Micro-Cooker®** on HIGH 30 seconds or until melted. Pour preserves over fruit, tossing gently. Spoon fruit mixture evenly over filling.

5. Pipe topping across top of pastry in lattice pattern (see Cook's Tip). Pipe a decorative border around edge. Sprinkle with Spice Blend. Garnish with mint, if desired. Cut into wedges using **Chef's Knife**.

Yield: 12 servings

Nutrients per serving: Calories 340, Total Fat 18 g, Saturated Fat 8.5 g, Cholesterol 15 mg, Carbohydrate 40 g, Protein 4 g, Sodium 210 mg, Fiber 2 g
Diabetic exchanges per serving: 1 Starch, 1 1/2 Fruit, 3 Fat (2 1/2 Carb, 3 Fat)

# Decadent Chocolate Cake

*Pictured on p. 69*

*Like most flourless chocolate cakes, this one is intensely rich. If you're a person who can never get enough chocolate, try this dessert.*

**Crust**
- 20   chocolate wafers, finely crushed (about 1 cup)
- 3   tablespoons butter, melted

**Cake**
- 12   squares (1 ounce each) semi-sweet chocolate for baking
- 3/4   cup butter
- 6   eggs, separated
- 12   tablespoons granulated sugar, divided
- 2   teaspoons vanilla

**Glaze and Garnish (page 68)**

1. Preheat oven to 350°F. Lightly spray **Springform Pan** with nonstick cooking spray. For crust, finely crush chocolate wafers in resealable plastic bag with **Baker's Roller™**. Microwave butter in **Small Micro-Cooker®** on HIGH 30 seconds or until melted. Stir in crumbs; mix well. Press crumb mixture onto bottom of pan.

2. For cake, melt chocolate and butter in **Small (2-qt.) Saucepan** over very low heat stirring occasionally with **Nylon Spiral Whisk** until smooth. Remove from heat. Cool slightly, stirring occasionally.

3. Using **Egg Separator**, separate egg whites into **Small Batter Bowl**; set aside. Place egg yolks in **Classic Batter Bowl**. On high speed of electric mixer, beat egg yolks and 6 tablespoons of the sugar until mixture is very thick and pale, about 3 minutes. Add cooled chocolate mixture; beat on low speed. Blend in vanilla.

4. Using clean, dry beaters, beat egg whites until soft peaks forms. Gradually add remaining 6 tablespoons sugar, 1 tablespoon at a time, beating until stiff peaks form. Using **Mix 'N Scraper®**, fold egg whites into chocolate mixture until well blended. Pour batter into pan.

5. Bake 45-50 minutes or until top is puffed and cracked. (**Cake Tester** inserted in center comes out with some moist crumbs attached.) Cool completely on **Nonstick Cooling Rack**. Run knife around sides of pan to loosen cake. Release collar from pan.

*(Continued on page 68)*

## Kitchen Tips

**Prep time:** 30 minutes
**Bake time:** 45-50 minutes
**Cool time:** 2 hours
**Chill time:** 30 minutes

### Cook's Tips

▲ To achieve maximum volume when beating egg whites, it's very important to start with a clean, dry bowl and beaters. Be sure no egg yolk is mixed with the whites. Equally important is to add the sugar *gradually* while beating whites.

▲ When beating egg whites, soft peaks are peaks that are rounded or curled under when beaters are lifted from the bowl. Stiff peaks stand up straight when beaters are lifted.

# Kitchen Tips

## Cook's Tip

▲ For a simpler garnish, omit chocolate pieces in Step 7 and sprinkle cake with powdered sugar or unsweetened cocoa powder just before serving.

## Make-Ahead Tip

▲ Unglazed cake can be made a day in advance and stored, covered, in the refrigerator. Bring cake to room temperature to glaze and garnish up to several hours before serving.

### Glaze

- **6 squares (1 ounce each) semi-sweet chocolate for baking**
- **2 tablespoons butter**
- **3 tablespoons milk**
- **2 tablespoons light corn syrup**

### Garnish (optional)

- **3 squares (1 ounce each) semi-sweet chocolate for baking**
- **Powdered sugar (optional)**

6. Place sheet of **Parchment Paper** under cooling rack. For glaze, melt chocolate and butter in clean saucepan over very low heat, stirring occasionally until smooth. Remove pan from heat; stir in milk and corn syrup. Spread glaze smoothly over top and sides of cake using **Skinny Scraper**. Refrigerate until glaze is almost set, about 30 minutes, before garnishing.

7. Meanwhile, for garnish, line **Chillzanne® Platter** with parchment paper. Place chocolate in **Small Micro-Cooker®**. Microwave on HIGH, uncovered, 1-1½ minutes or until melted, stirring every 30 seconds. Pour onto parchment and spread to a 10-inch circle. Place in freezer 5 minutes to firm. Break chocolate into large pieces; sprinkle top of cake and chocolate pieces with powdered sugar, if desired. Arrange chocolate pieces randomly over top of cake, lightly pressing into glaze and cake. Refrigerate up to 1 hour before serving. Cut into slices.

Yield: 18 servings

Nutrients per serving: Calories 350, Total Fat 27 g, Saturated Fat 15 g, Cholesterol 100 mg, Carbohydrate 31 g, Protein 5 g, Sodium 190 mg, Fiber 1 g
Diabetic exchanges per serving: 2 Starch, 5 Fat (2 Carb, 5 Fat)

# Macadamia Key Lime Pie

*Guests will delight in this cool and refreshing pie.*
*Buttery-rich macadamia nuts give the crust added flavor and crunch.*

### Crust
- 1/2   package (15 ounces) refrigerated pie crusts (1 crust)
- 1/2   cup plus 1 tablespoon macadamia nuts, coarsely chopped, divided

### Filling
- 4   large limes
- 1   package (8 ounces) cream cheese, softened
- 1   can (14 ounces) sweetened condensed milk (not evaporated milk)
- 3-4   drops *each* green and yellow food coloring (optional)
- 1   container (12 ounces) frozen whipped topping, thawed, divided

Additional lime slices, for garnish

1. Preheat oven to 450°F. For crust, let pie crust stand at room temperature 15 minutes. Gently unfold onto lightly floured surface. Roll to 11 1/2-inch circle using floured **Baker's Roller™**. Place crust in **Deep Dish Pie Plate**, pressing dough into bottom and up sides. Prick bottom and sides using pastry tool.

2. Coarsely chop nuts with **Food Chopper**. Sprinkle 1/2 cup of the nuts over bottom of pie crust. Bake 10-11 minutes or until crust is golden brown. Cool completely.

3. For filling, zest limes with **Lemon Zester/Scorer** to measure 3 teaspoons zest. Juice limes to measure 1/2 cup juice. Combine cream cheese and sweetened condensed milk in **Classic Batter Bowl**; whisk until smooth using **Stainless Steel Whisk**. Stir zest, juice and food coloring into cream cheese mixture; mix well. Fold in 2 cups of the whipped topping using **Classic Scraper**. Pour mixture into crust. Refrigerate at least 30 minutes.

4. In **Small Sauté Pan**, toast remaining 1 tablespoon nuts over medium heat until light golden brown, stirring constantly. Remove nuts from pan and cool completely. Garnish top of pie with remaining whipped topping using **Easy Accent® Decorator** and lime slices, if desired. Sprinkle with nuts. Cut into wedges using **Slice 'N Serve®**.

Yield: 8 servings

Nutrients per serving: Calories 640, Total Fat 38 g, Saturated Fat 22 g, Cholesterol 60 mg, Carbohydrate 63 g, Protein 9 g, Sodium 270 mg, Fiber 1 g
Diabetic exchanges per serving: 2 Starch, 2 Fruit, 7 Fat (4 Carb, 7 Fat)

## Kitchen Tips

**Prep time:** 30 minutes
**Bake time:** 10-11 minutes
**Cool time:** 30 minutes
**Chill time:** 30 minutes

### Cook's Tips

▲ Persian limes are the most common limes available in the supermarket and provide excellent results in this recipe. Fresh Key limes are grown in Florida and the Caribbean and are not available in most areas of the country, but can be substituted for the Persian limes, if you like. Bottled Key lime juice can be used as well, but don't omit lime zest. Key limes are smaller, rounder and tarter than Persian limes and have a yellow tint to the peel and flesh.

▲ Wash and dry limes before removing zest. Limes will release the most juice if they are at room temperature. You can warm refrigerated limes in the microwave oven on HIGH for about 10 seconds before juicing.

Prep time: 45 minutes
Bake time: 60-65 minutes
Cool time: 1 hour
Chill time: 1 hour

### Cook's Tip

▲ You can substitute preserves for the jam, but if there are large pieces of fruit, snip into small pieces with the **Kitchen Shears**. Lemon curd makes another tasty filling for this cake; however, you'll want to omit the almond extract in the cake.

### Tool Tips

▲ To easily cut cake horizontally in half, use 8-10 wooden picks to mark the middle point on the sides, all around the cake. Using the **Serrated Bread Knife**, cut through cake just above the picks.

▲ The **Deep Dish Baker** can be substituted for the Springform Pan. Bake cake 40-45 minutes. Proceed as recipe directs.

# Coconut Cake

*Making this traditional layer cake just got simpler with a dreamy frosting made with a white chocolate pudding mix.*

**Cake**
- 1 package (18.25 ounces) white cake mix (plus ingredients to make cake)
- 1 teaspoon almond extract

**Frosting & Filling**
- 3/4 cup cold milk
- 1 package (3.3 ounces) white chocolate instant pudding and pie filling
- 1/4 cup powdered sugar
- 1 container (8 ounces) frozen whipped topping, thawed
- 1/3 cup cherry or peach jam
- 1 cup sweetened flaked coconut

1. Preheat oven to 325°F. Cut a circle of **Parchment Paper** to fit flat bottom of **Springform Pan**. Spray pan with nonstick cooking spray; place parchment circle on bottom.

2. For cake, in **Classic Batter Bowl**, prepare cake mix according to package directions adding almond extract with water; pour batter into pan. Bake 60-65 minutes or until **Cake Tester** inserted in center comes out clean. Cool on **Nonstick Cooling Rack** 10 minutes. Run knife around edge of cake and release collar of pan. Cool cake completely.

3. Place cooling rack over top of cake; invert and remove bottom of pan and parchment. Invert cake to serving plate. Cut cake in half horizontally. Gently slide top half onto **Cutting Board**.

4. For frosting, pour milk into clean Batter Bowl. Add pudding mix and powdered sugar. Whisk 1-2 minutes or until pudding begins to thicken. Fold in whipped topping.

5. To assemble cake, spread jam over bottom half of cake using **Large Spreader**. Spread 1 cup of the frosting over jam. Top with remaining cake layer. Spread sides and top of cake with remaining frosting. Gently pat coconut over cake. Refrigerate 1 hour. Serve using **Slice 'N Serve®**.

Yield: 16 servings

Nutrients per serving: Calories 280, Total Fat 10 g, Saturated Fat 5 g, Cholesterol 0 mg, Carbohydrate 43 g, Protein 3 g, Sodium 330 mg, Fiber less than 1 g
Diabetic exchanges per serving: 1 Starch, 2 Fruit, 2 Fat (3 Carb, 1 1/2 Fat)

# Almond Puff Pastry with Glazed Plums

*Create this elegant pastry with the help of convenient frozen puff pastry sheets.*

**Pastry**
- 1 **cup slivered almonds, finely ground**
- 3 **tablespoons sugar**
- 2 **tablespoons all-purpose flour**
- 1 **package (17.3 ounces) frozen puff pastry sheets, thawed**

**Fruit Topping**
- 4 **red plums (about 1 pound)**
- 4 **purple plums (about 1 pound)**
- 2 **tablespoons sugar**
- 1 **teaspoon Pantry Cinnamon Plus™ Spice Blend**
- 1/3 **cup plum preserves**
  **Vanilla ice cream or whipped cream (optional)**

1. Preheat oven to 400°F. For pastry, place almonds in **Deluxe Cheese Grater** and finely grate into **Small Batter Bowl**. Add sugar and flour; mix thoroughly and set aside.

2. Unfold puff pastry sheets. To cover **Rectangle Stone** with puff pastry, start by placing sheets at top edge of Baking Stone, overlapping ½ inch in center. (Fold lines of pastry will be parallel to long side of Baking Stone. Pastry will extend beyond short sides of Baking Stone on both sides.) Cut off pastry extending beyond Baking Stone and place at bottom to finish covering Stone, overlapping about ½ inch at all seams. Discard any extra pastry. Roll pastry firmly with **Baker's Roller™** to seal all seams. Trim off corners to fit Baking Stone, if necessary. Prick entire surface (including seam areas) with pastry tool.

3. Spread almond mixture evenly over pastry to within ½ inch of edge. Bake 15 minutes or until pastry is slightly puffed and begins to turn golden. Remove from oven to **Nonstick Cooling Rack**.

4. Meanwhile, for fruit topping, remove pits from plums with **The Corer™**. Slice into rings using v-shaped blade of **Ultimate Slice & Grate**. Stack the slices of each plum and cut in half. Combine sugar and Spice Blend in **Flour/Sugar Shaker**; set aside.

5. Arrange plum slices in six rows along the width of the pastry, keeping colors separated and in alternate rows. Sprinkle sugar mixture over plums. Return pastry to oven and continue baking 15 minutes or until pastry is browned and plums are soft.

6. Microwave preserves in **Small Micro-Cooker®** on HIGH 30 seconds or until melted. Brush over plums using **Pastry Brush**. Cool at least 10 minutes. Cut pastry into squares. Serve warm or at room temperature with ice cream, if desired.

Yield: 20 squares

Nutrients per serving (1 square): Calories 230, Total Fat 13 g, Saturated Fat 2.5 g, Cholesterol 0 mg, Carbohydrate 26 g, Protein 4 g, Sodium 65 mg, Fiber 2 g
Diabetic exchanges per serving (1 square): 2 Starch, 2 Fat (2 Carb, 2 Fat)

**Prep time: 40 minutes**
**Bake time: 30 minutes**
**Cool time: 10 minutes**

### Cook's Tips

▲ Thaw puff pastry sheets at room temperature about 30 minutes before using.

▲ Substitute pumpkin pie spice or ground cinnamon for Cinnamon Plus™ Spice Blend, if desired.

▲ When arranging plum slices in rows, alternate the direction of the slices to give dessert added interest.

▲ You'll find plums are most plentiful from mid-summer through early fall. It's best to use slightly firm plums that have just started to ripen. Plums should be plump and yield slightly to gentle pressure. To ripen plums at home, store them for 1-2 days in a closed paper bag at room temperature.

## Kitchen Tips

Prep time: 30 minutes
Bake time: 30-35 minutes
Cool time: 1 hour

### Cook's Tip

▲ For *Chocolate Mousse Cake Roll*, prepare cake according to recipe directions in Steps 1 and 2. Unroll cake; discard parchment. Combine 1 package (8 ounces) cream cheese, softened, 1/3 cup powdered sugar, 3 tablespoons unsweetened cocoa powder and 1 tablespoon milk; mix well. Fold in 1 cup thawed whipped topping; gently spread over cake to within 1 inch of edge; re-roll cake. Sprinkle with additional powdered sugar. Slice and serve with additional whipped topping and chocolate sauce.

# Luscious Lemon Angel Roll

*This elegant dessert features a refreshing lemon filling and strawberry topping all swirled in a light and airy angel food cake.*

1 package (16 ounces) angel food cake mix
3/4 cup powdered sugar, divided
1 jar (11.75 ounces) strawberry ice cream topping, divided
1 package (8 ounces) cream cheese, softened
1 lemon
7 drops yellow food coloring (optional)
1 container (8 ounces) frozen light whipped topping, thawed, divided
Powdered sugar
12 whole strawberries with stems and lemon slices, for garnish

1. Preheat oven to 350°F. Cut an 18-inch long piece of **Parchment Paper**. Press into bottom and up sides of **Stoneware Bar Pan**. Prepare cake mix according to package directions; pour batter over parchment, spreading evenly. Bake 30-35 minutes or until top springs back when lightly touched with fingertip. Remove from oven to **Nonstick Cooling Rack**.

2. Sprinkle 1/2 cup of the powdered sugar over cake using **Flour/Sugar Shaker**. Place a sheet of parchment over cake. Place cooling rack upside down over parchment and carefully turn cake out at once. Remove pan and parchment from bottom of cake. Starting at one short side, roll up cake in parchment. Cool completely.

3. Unroll cake and transfer to **Large Grooved Cutting Board**; discard parchment. Spread cake with 1/4 cup of the ice cream topping, pressing lightly using **Skinny Scraper**. Combine cream cheese and remaining 1/4 cup powdered sugar in **Classic Batter Bowl**; mix well. Zest lemon using **Lemon Zester/Scorer**; juice lemon to measure 1 tablespoon juice. Add zest and juice to cream cheese mixture; whisk using **Stainless Steel Whisk**. Add food coloring, if desired; mix well. Fold in 1 cup of the whipped topping; gently spread over ice cream topping to within 1 inch of edge; re-roll cake.

4. Sprinkle with additional powdered sugar. Slice using **Serrated Bread Knife**. Attach open star tip to **Easy Accent® Decorator**; fill with remaining whipped topping. Garnish each serving with whipped topping, strawberry fan, lemon slice and remaining ice cream topping.

Yield: 12 servings

Nutrients per serving: Calories 360, Total Fat 9 g, Saturated Fat 6 g, Cholesterol 20 mg, Carbohydrate 64 g, Sodium 400 mg, Dietary Fiber 0 g
Diabetic exchanges per serving: 1 Starch, 3 Fruit, 2 Fat (4 Carb, 1 Fat)

### Cook's Tips

▲ Strawberries must be very dry before dipping into white chocolate; even a drop of water can cause the chocolate to become grainy.

▲ Vanilla instant pudding and pie filling can be substituted for the white chocolate pudding, if desired.

▲ Garnish top of the blueberries with lemon zest using **Lemon Zester/Scorer**, if desired.

### Tool Tip

▲ Rinse and drain blueberries in the small **Colander**, just one of two colanders in the **4-Piece Colander & Bowl Set**. While the small colander is perfect for draining tuna, fruits and vegetables, the large colander is great for draining cooked pasta and rinsing salad greens. Two nesting bowls are also included in the set.

# Red, White & Blueberry Pie

*Show your patriotic spirit with a glorious pie
as American as apple.*

| | |
|---|---|
| ½ | **package (15 ounces) refrigerated pie crusts (1 crust)** |
| 1 | **quart fresh strawberries, divided** |
| 4 | **squares (1 ounce each) white chocolate for baking** |
| 1 | **package (8 ounces) reduced-fat cream cheese (Neufchâtel), softened** |
| ¾ | **cup cold milk** |
| 1 | **package (3.3 ounces) white chocolate instant pudding and pie filling** |
| 1½ | **cups fresh blueberries** |
| 1 | **cup thawed, frozen light whipped topping** |

1. Preheat oven to 425°F. Let pie crust stand at room temperature 15 minutes. Gently unfold onto lightly floured surface. Roll to 11½-inch circle using floured **Baker's Roller™**. Place crust in **Deep Dish Pie Plate**, pressing dough into bottom and up sides. Prick bottom and sides using pastry tool. Bake 10-12 minutes or until golden brown. Cool completely.

2. Rinse strawberries and pat dry on paper towels. Select 8 uniformly sized strawberries for dipping; cut in half through stem ends using **Paring Knife**. Set aside. Hull and slice remaining strawberries using **Egg Slicer Plus®**.

3. Melt white chocolate in **Small Micro-Cooker®**, uncovered, on HIGH 1 minute, stirring every 10 seconds, until chocolate is melted and smooth. Do not overheat. Dip strawberry halves in melted chocolate; place on a sheet of **Parchment Paper**, cut side down. Refrigerate 15 minutes or until set.

4. Using **Skinny Scraper**, scrape remaining melted chocolate over bottom of prepared pie crust, spreading evenly to coat entire bottom and sides of crust. Layer sliced strawberries over bottom of crust.

5. Beat cream cheese in **Classic Batter Bowl** with **Stainless Steel Whisk** until smooth. Gradually whisk in milk until well blended. Add pudding mix; whisk until mixture begins to thicken. Spread mixture evenly over strawberries using **Classic Scraper**.

6. Arrange blueberries evenly over top of pie filling. Attach open star tip to **Easy Accent® Decorator** and fill with whipped topping. Pipe topping evenly around edge of pie. Place dipped strawberry halves on whipped topping border. Refrigerate until ready to serve. Cut into wedges using **Slice 'N Serve®**.

Yield: 8 servings

Nutrients per serving: Calories 370, Total Fat 20 g, Saturated Fat 11 g, Cholesterol 30 mg, Carbohydrate 44 g, Protein 6 g, Sodium 290 mg, Dietary Fiber 2 g
Diabetic exchanges per serving: 2 Starch, 1 Fruit, 3½ Fat (3 Carb, 3 Fat)

# Lace Baskets with Ice Cream

*These delicate dessert cups are reminiscent of Southern pralines.*

1/3 cup packed brown sugar
1/4 cup butter or margarine (do not use stick vegetable oil spread)
1/4 cup light corn syrup
1/2 cup finely chopped nuts
1/3 cup all-purpose flour
1 quart ice cream, any flavor
Fresh berries, ice cream topping or *Spiced Apple Topping* (optional)

1. Preheat oven to 350°F. Combine brown sugar, butter and corn syrup in **Small (2-qt.) Saucepan**. Heat over medium-low heat until sugar is dissolved, stirring occasionally with **Nylon Spiral Whisk**. Remove pan from heat; stir in nuts and flour.

2. Cut two 15-inch circles of **Parchment Paper**. Place one circle on **Large Round Stone**. Using **Medium Scoop**, drop 4 level scoops of batter, 3 inches apart, onto parchment. (Batter will spread while baking.)

3. Bake 18-19 minutes or until deep golden brown. Slide parchment onto **Nonstick Cooling Rack**. Cool 30-60 seconds. Turn **Stoneware Muffin Pan** upside down. Using **Large Serving Spatula**, quickly remove one cookie and carefully place over bottom side of cup; gently form into a basket. Repeat with remaining cookies. Cool 2 minutes; remove from muffin pan to cooling rack. Cool completely.

4. Scoop remaining batter onto second parchment circle; place on hot Baking Stone. Bake 9-10 minutes or until deep golden brown. Repeat method in Step 3 to form baskets.

5. For each serving, scoop ice cream into lace basket. Top with fresh berries, ice cream topping or *Spiced Apple Topping*, if desired.

Yield: 8 servings

Nutrients per serving: Calories 310, Total Fat 18 g, Saturated Fat 9 g, Cholesterol 45 mg, Carbohydrate 38 g, Protein 3 g, Sodium 130 mg, Fiber less than 1 g
Diabetic exchanges per serving: 1 Starch, 1 1/2 Fruit, 3 Fat (2 1/2 Carb, 3 Fat)

## Spiced Apple Topping

3 medium Jonathan or Braeburn apples (about 1 1/4 pounds)
1/3 cup packed brown sugar
3/4 teaspoon Pantry Cinnamon Plus™ Spice Blend
1/3 cup apple juice
1 tablespoon cornstarch
2 tablespoons butter or margarine

1. Core and slice apples with **Apple Peeler/Corer/Slicer** (do not peel); cut apples in half. Combine brown sugar and Spice Blend; set aside. Whisk apple juice with cornstarch; set aside.

2. Melt butter in **Stir-Fry Skillet** over medium heat. Add apples; stir-fry 2 minutes. Stir in brown sugar mixture and continue stir-frying 2 minutes. Stir in juice mixture; bring to a boil. Cook 1 minute, stirring constantly, until sauce is thickened. Serve warm over ice cream, crepes, pancakes or waffles.

Yield: About 2 cups

LOW FAT

Nutrients per serving (about 1/4 cup): Calories 100, Total Fat 3 g, Saturated Fat 2 g, Cholesterol 10 mg, Carbohydrate 19 g, Protein 0 g, Sodium 35 mg, Fiber 1 g
Diabetic exchanges per serving: 1 Fruit, 1/2 Fat (1 Carb, 1/2 Fat)

## Kitchen Tips

Prep time: 30 minutes
Bake time: 27-29 minutes
Cool time: 30 minutes

### Cook's Tips

▲ Less time is required to bake the second batch of cookies because the Baking Stone is already hot. These cookies need to be baked until deep golden brown; otherwise, baskets will not have a crisp texture.

▲ When shaping cookies into baskets, if the cookies become too hard to mold around the muffin cups, return them to the warm Baking Stone to soften.

### Make-Ahead Tip

▲ Lace baskets can be baked ahead and stored up to 1 week in a tightly covered container.

### Tool Tip

▲ Use the **Food Chopper** to finely chop nuts.

# Pink Lemonade Ice Cream Cake

*Treat your friends to a sweet taste of summer any day of the year.*

**Crust**
- 51 reduced-fat vanilla wafers, divided
- 3 tablespoons stick vegetable oil spread (70% fat), melted

**Filling**
- 2 cups fat-free, no sugar added vanilla ice cream, softened
- 1 can (6 ounces) frozen pink lemonade concentrate, thawed (3/4 cup)
- 1 container (12 ounces) frozen fat-free whipped topping, thawed, divided

**Garnish (optional)**
- Lemon slices
- Pink sugar crystals
- Mint leaves

1. Lightly spray **Springform Pan** with nonstick cooking spray. For crust, place 32 of the wafers in resealable plastic bag; crush into fine crumbs using **Baker's Roller™**. Place crumbs in **Small Batter Bowl**. Add melted vegetable oil spread; mix well. Press crumb mixture into bottom of pan. Line inside of pan with remaining wafers, slightly overlapping and with rounded side of wafers next to collar.

2. For filling, combine ice cream and lemonade concentrate in **Classic Batter Bowl**. Beat until smooth with **Stainless Steel Whisk**. Fold in 3 cups of the whipped topping using **Classic Scraper**. Pour mixture into crust. Freeze until firm, at least 3 hours.

3. When ready to serve, place dessert in refrigerator 15 minutes before slicing.

4. Run **Utility Knife** around sides of dessert. Release collar from pan. Garnish top with remaining whipped topping using **Easy Accent® Decorator**. Add sugared lemon twists and mint, if desired.

Yield: 16 servings

LOW FAT | Nutrients per serving: Calories 140, Total Fat 3 g, Saturated Fat 0 g, Cholesterol 0 mg, Carbohydrate 26 g, Protein 1 g, Sodium 95 mg, Fiber 0 g
Diabetic exchanges per serving: 1 Starch, 1 Fruit (2 Carb)

Prep time: 20 minutes
Bake time: 1 hour
Cool time: 30-60 minutes

## Cook's Tips

▲ Substitute 1/4 teaspoon cream of tartar for vinegar, if desired. Vinegar or cream of tartar helps to stabilize the egg whites.

▲ For best results, choose a cool, dry day for making meringue shells.

▲ To substitute whipped cream for the whipped topping, whip 1 1/2 cups whipping cream with 2-3 tablespoons powdered sugar until stiff peaks form.

## Tool Tip

▲ While eggs are still cold, separate with the **Egg Separator** that conveniently attaches to the Classic Batter Bowl. Eggs separate best when at refrigerated temperature, but egg whites beat to their fullest volume at room temperature. Don't let even a speck of yolk get into whites.

# Cocoa Meringue Shells

*While individual shells are a beautiful finale to any fine meal, don't miss our variation for Cocoa Meringue Kisses—a sweet gift-giving idea for any occasion.*

**Shells**

- 1 1/2  teaspoons cornstarch
- 1 1/2  teaspoons raspberry vinegar
- 3  large egg whites
- 3/4  cup granulated sugar
- 3  tablespoons unsweetened cocoa powder

**Filling**

- 1  container (8 ounces) frozen fat-free or light whipped topping, thawed
- 1  pint raspberries
  Fresh mint leaves (optional)

1. Preheat oven to 275°F. For shells, whisk together cornstarch and vinegar and set aside. In **Classic Batter Bowl**, beat egg whites on high speed of electric mixer just until very foamy, about 20 seconds. Add cornstarch mixture and continue to beat until soft peaks form, 1-2 minutes. (Tips of peaks will curl down when beaters are lifted.) Then, in a slow steady stream, gradually add sugar. (Do not add all of the sugar at once.) Continue beating on high speed until sugar is dissolved, mixture is glossy and stiff peaks form, 3-4 minutes. (Tips of peaks will remain upright when beaters are lifted.)

2. Place cocoa powder in **Flour/Sugar Shaker**; sprinkle over egg whites while gently folding with **Classic Scraper** until thoroughly combined.

3. Cover **Rectangle Stone** with piece of **Parchment Paper**. Draw six 3-inch circles with pencil, spacing evenly. Fit **Easy Accent® Decorator** with closed star tip and fill with meringue mixture. Pipe mixture (about 1/2 inch high) onto circles to form bases for shells. Smooth with **All-Purpose Spreader**. Pipe a decorative border around each base to create sides.

4. Bake 1 hour. Meringue shells should be dry and have small cracks. Turn oven off and leave shells in oven with door slightly ajar for 30-60 minutes or until shells are thoroughly dry.

5. When ready to serve, for filling, fit clean decorator with open star tip and fill with whipped topping. Pipe into shells and top with raspberries. Garnish with mint leaves.

Yield: 6 servings

**LOW FAT** Nutrients per serving: Calories 200, Total Fat .5 g, Saturated Fat 0 g, Cholesterol 0 mg, Carbohydrate 45 g, Protein 3 g, Sodium 50 mg, Fiber 2 g
Diabetic exchanges per serving: 1 Starch, 2 Fruit (3 Carb)

***Variations: Large Cocoa Meringue Shell:*** Draw 9-inch circle on parchment paper. Pipe mixture to form large shell. Bake and fill as recipe directs. Cut into wedges using **Slice 'N Serve®**.

**Cocoa Meringue Kisses:** Using open star tip, pipe mixture into small rosettes, 1 inch apart, on parchment paper. Bake as recipe directs. Store in tightly covered container. Makes about 6 dozen cookies.

### Make-Ahead Tip

▲ This dessert can be assembled and refrigerated several hours before being served. It can even be unmolded, frosted and garnished 1-2 hours before serving. Just be sure to keep dessert refrigerated.

### Tool Tip

▲ Creating a strawberry fan is easy using the **Egg Slicer Plus®**. Open and place the strawberry stem end down; slice most of the way through it with wires. Carefully remove strawberry from wires and fan out slices.

# Strawberries & Cream Cloud

*Light and dreamy, this frosted dome of glazed strawberries,*
*fluffy vanilla filling and angel food cake is a dessert anyone can enjoy.*

2  cups sliced strawberries
1/2  cup light sugar-free strawberry preserves
1  ready prepared angel food cake (12-13 ounces)
1  container (8 ounces) vanilla low-fat yogurt
1/4  cup fat-free (skim) milk
1  package (1 ounce) vanilla sugar-free instant pudding and pie filling
1  container (12 ounces) frozen light whipped topping, thawed, divided
9  whole strawberries with stems, for garnish

1. Slice strawberries using **Egg Slicer Plus®**. Gently mix with strawberry preserves in **Small Batter Bowl**; set aside.

2. Slice angel food cake into twenty 1/2-inch slices using **Serrated Bread Knife**. Line **Chillzanne® Bowl** with plastic wrap.

3. In **Classic Batter Bowl**, combine yogurt and milk using **Stainless Steel Whisk**. Whisk in pudding mix until mixture begins to thicken. Stir in 2 cups of the whipped topping. Refrigerate remaining whipped topping.

4. To assemble dessert, cover bottom of Chillzanne® Bowl with 5 cake slices. Layer half of the strawberry mixture evenly over cake slices; spread with half of the pudding mixture. Cover with 7 cake slices, pressing lightly. Repeat layers with remaining strawberry and pudding mixtures. Cover with remaining 8 cake slices, pressing lightly. Cover and refrigerate at least 2 hours.

5. To serve, invert dessert onto serving plate; remove plastic wrap. Using **All-Purpose Spreader**, frost with remaining whipped topping. Reserve 1 strawberry for creating a fan (see Tool Tip). Cut remaining strawberries in half through stem ends. Place strawberry halves stem ends down evenly around bottom edge of dessert. Top with strawberry fan. Cut into wedges with **Slice 'N Serve®**.

Yield: 16 servings

LOW FAT  Nutrients per serving: Calories 140, Total Fat 3 g, Saturated Fat 3 g, Cholesterol 0 mg, Carbohydrate 26 g, Protein 2 g, Sodium 190 mg, Fiber 0 g
Diabetic exchanges per serving: 1 Starch, 1 Fruit (2 Carb)

# Black Bottom Banana Cream Pie

*Marrying the flavors of two traditional pies led to the creation of this recipe,*
*and happiness ever after.*

½ **package (15 ounces) refrigerated pie crusts (1 crust)**
1 **container (12 ounces) frozen whipped topping, thawed, divided**
1 **package (6 ounces) semi-sweet chocolate morsels**
1½ **cups cold milk**
1 **package (5.1 ounces) vanilla instant pudding and pie filling (6 servings)**
½ **teaspoon rum extract (optional)**
2 **medium bananas, sliced, divided**
**Strawberries for garnish**

1. Preheat oven to 425°F. Let pie crust stand at room temperature 15 minutes. Gently unfold onto lightly floured surface. Roll to 11½-inch circle using floured **Baker's Roller™**. Place crust in **Deep Dish Pie Plate**, pressing dough into bottom and up sides. Prick bottom and sides using pastry tool. Bake 10-12 minutes or until golden brown. Cool completely.

2. Place 1½ cups of the whipped topping and chocolate morsels in **Small Micro-Cooker®**. Microwave, uncovered, on HIGH 30-45 seconds; stir until smooth. Remove 2 tablespoons of the chocolate mixture to a small, resealable plastic bag for garnishing; set aside. Spread remaining chocolate mixture over bottom of pie crust using **All-Purpose Spreader**. Place crust in freezer while preparing pudding.

3. Pour milk into **Classic Batter Bowl**. Add pudding mix and rum extract; whisk 1 minute or until mixture begins to thicken. Fold in 1½ cups of the whipped topping.

4. Slice 1½ bananas; arrange slices over chocolate mixture in crust. Spread pudding mixture over bananas. Refrigerate 30 minutes.

5. To garnish pie, cut small tip off corner of plastic bag filled with chocolate mixture. Squeeze chocolate mixture over pie in decorative design. Fill **Easy Accent® Decorator** with remaining whipped topping. Pipe rosettes at edge of pie. Garnish with remaining ½ banana and strawberries, sliced. Cut pie into wedges.

Yield: 8 servings

Nutrients per serving: Calories 470, Total Fat 22 g, Saturated Fat 14 g, Cholesterol 10 mg, Carbohydrate 63 g, Protein 3 g, Sodium 380 mg, Fiber less than 1 g
Diabetic exchanges per serving: 2 Starch, 3 Fruit, 4 Fat (4 Carb, 3½ Fat)

## Kitchen Tips

Prep time: 40 minutes
Bake time: 10-12 minutes
Cool time: 30 minutes
Chill time: 30 minutes

### Cook's Tips

▲ For a colder serving temperature and easier cutting, refrigerate pie 1-2 hours.

▲ When placing refrigerated pie crust in the Deep Dish Pie Plate, evenly ruffle edge of crust inside pie plate for picture-perfect results. To keep crust from slipping down sides of pie plate during baking, firmly press edge of pie crust to fluted edge of pie plate in several places.

### Tool Tips

▲ When preparing the chocolate garnish, it's handy to place the resealable plastic bag inside a **Measure-All® Cup** before filling it with the chocolate mixture.

▲ Use the **Egg Slicer Plus®** for slicing the bananas and strawberries.

Prep time: 30 minutes
Bake time: 30-35 minutes
Cool time: 1 hour
Freeze time: 4 hours

## Cook's Tip

▲ Substitute 1¹/₂ squares (1¹/₂ ounces) semi-sweet chocolate for baking for chocolate morsels, if desired.

## Tool Tip

▲ Use the **Easy Accent® Decorator** to pipe a pretty rosette of whipped topping onto each slice of *Tiramisu Ice Cream Cake*. With six decorating tips, it's the perfect garnishing tool for use with whipped cream and topping, frosting, meringue and soft fillings.

# Tiramisu Ice Cream Cake

*We've put a twist on the popular Italian dessert, tiramisu, and made the most heavenly coffee and chocolate ice cream dessert ever.*

1 package (16 ounces) angel food cake mix
3 tablespoons unsweetened cocoa powder, divided
1 quart coffee ice cream
4 teaspoons instant coffee granules
¹/₄ cup hot water
¹/₃ cup powdered sugar
¹/₄ cup semi-sweet chocolate morsels
1¹/₂ cups thawed, frozen whipped topping

1. Preheat oven to 350°F. Cut an 18-inch long piece of **Parchment Paper**. Press into bottom and up sides of **Stoneware Bar Pan**. Prepare cake mix according to package directions; pour batter over parchment, spreading evenly using **Classic Scraper**. Bake 30-35 minutes or until top springs back when lightly touched with fingertip. Remove from oven to **Nonstick Cooling Rack**.

2. Sprinkle 2 tablespoons of the cocoa powder over cake using **Flour/Sugar Shaker**. Place a sheet of parchment over cake. Place cooling rack upside down over parchment and carefully turn cake out at once. Remove pan and parchment from bottom of cake. Starting at one short side, roll up cake in parchment. Cool completely.

3. Soften ice cream in refrigerator 20 minutes. In **Small Batter Bowl**, whisk coffee granules and remaining 1 tablespoon cocoa powder into hot water until dissolved using **Stainless Steel Whisk**. Whisk in powdered sugar until completely blended.

4. Unroll cake; leave on parchment. Using **Pastry Brush**, brush cake with coffee mixture. Place chocolate morsels in **Deluxe Cheese Grater**; grate evenly over cake. Using **Ice Cream Dipper**, scoop ice cream over grated chocolate; spread evenly to within 1 inch of edges using **Large Spreader**. Re-roll cake, removing parchment as you roll. Wrap cake in heavy-duty aluminum foil. Freeze until firm, at least 4 hours.

5. When ready to serve, let wrapped cake roll stand at room temperature 10-20 minutes to soften. Cut into 1-inch slices using **Serrated Bread Knife**. Garnish slices with whipped topping and additional grated chocolate or cocoa powder.

Yield: 12 servings

Nutrients per serving: Calories 380, Total Fat 15 g, Saturated Fat 9 g, Cholesterol 80 mg, Carbohydrate 55 g, Protein 7 g, Sodium 340 mg, Fiber less than 1 g
Diabetic exchanges per serving: 2 Starch, 2 Fruit, 2¹/₂ Fat (4 Carb, 2 Fat)

*Variation:* **Slim 'n Trim Tiramisu Cake Roll:** Substitute fat-free vanilla ice cream for coffee ice cream and light whipped topping for the regular whipped topping.

LOW FAT   Nutrients per serving: Calories 260, Total Fat 2.5 g, Saturated Fat 1.5 g, Cholesterol 0 mg, Carbohydrate 54 g, Protein 6 g, Sodium 320 mg, Fiber less than 1 g
Diabetic exchanges per serving: 2 Starch, 2 Fruit (4 Carb)

**Prep time:** 25 minutes
**Bake time:** 55-60 minutes
**Cool time:** 2 hours
**Chill time:** 4 hours

### Cook's Tips

▲ For a cheesecake with the creamiest texture, bring ingredients to room temperature before beginning. Place eggs in a bowl of warm water for about 10 minutes and microwave cream cheese in the Classic Batter Bowl on HIGH 1 minute to soften.

▲ To prevent overbaking, always check cheesecakes at the minimum baking time given. When done, a center area about 1 inch in diameter will still jiggle slightly. The center will firm as it cools.

### Tool Tips

▲ Zest lemon with the **Lemon Zester/Scorer**, then finely chop zest with the **Food Chopper**.

▲ For a smooth cut, dip the **Utility Knife** into warm water and wipe it dry after each cut.

# New York-Style Cheesecake

*Just a hint of lemon flavors this truly classic dessert.*

**Crust**

26 regular size butter cookies (about 1¼ cups crushed)

4 tablespoons butter or margarine, divided

**Filling**

4 packages (8 ounces each) cream cheese, softened

1 cup sugar

3 tablespoons all-purpose flour

1 teaspoon lemon zest, finely chopped

1 tablespoon lemon juice

4 eggs, room temperature

½ cup sour cream

½ teaspoon vanilla

1 can (21 ounces) cherry or blueberry pie filling (optional)

1. Preheat oven to 325°F. For crust, place cookies in resealable plastic bag; crush into fine crumbs using **Baker's Roller**™. Melt 3 tablespoons of the butter in **Small Micro-Cooker®** on HIGH 30 seconds or until melted; add cookie crumbs and mix well.

2. Using **Pastry Brush**, brush sides of **Springform Pan** with remaining 1 tablespoon softened butter. Add crumb mixture. Tilt pan to lightly coat sides with crumb mixture. Press remaining loose crumb mixture into bottom of pan. Bake 8 minutes.

3. For filling, place cream cheese in **Classic Batter Bowl**. Add sugar, flour, lemon zest and juice. Beat at medium speed of electric mixer 3 minutes until well blended. Add eggs; mix at low speed 2 minutes. Blend in sour cream and vanilla using **Super Scraper**.

4. Pour filling into crust. Bake 55-60 minutes or until center appears nearly set when gently shaken. Remove from oven to **Nonstick Cooling Rack**. Immediately run **Quikut Paring Knife** around sides of cake to loosen from pan. Cool completely.

5. Release collar from pan. Refrigerate at least 4 hours or overnight. To serve, top with pie filling, if desired. Cut into wedges.

Yield: 12 servings

Nutrients per serving: Calories 480, Total Fat 38 g, Saturated Fat 20 g, Cholesterol 175 mg, Carbohydrate 28 g, Protein 9 g, Sodium 350 mg, Fiber 0 g
Diabetic exchanges per serving: 2 Starch, ½ Meat, 7 Fat (2 Carb, 7 Fat)

### Cook's Tips

▲ Phyllo dough is an ingredient found in many Greek and Middle Eastern recipes. It is available in supermarkets in the frozen foods section. Before using, thaw phyllo dough according to package directions, about 12 hours in the refrigerator.

▲ Keep phyllo sheets covered with plastic wrap while working on recipe. Otherwise, phyllo may dry out and crack, becoming unusable.

▲ These cups are versatile holders for pudding mixtures, ice cream or fruit.

▲ Ground cinnamon can be substituted for the Korintje Cinnamon, if desired.

# Phyllo Nests with Chocolate Mousse

*Impress your friends with these crispy dessert cups filled with a cinnamon-spiced chocolate cream.*

| | |
|---|---|
| 4 | sheets thawed, frozen phyllo dough (see Cook's Tip) |
| 1 | tablespoon granulated sugar |
| | Butter flavored nonstick cooking spray |
| 1 | package (2.8 ounces) European-style mousse mix, any flavor |
| 2/3 | cup cold fat-free (skim) milk |
| 1/4 | teaspoon Pantry Korintje Cinnamon |
| 1 1/2 | cups thawed, frozen light whipped topping |
| | Optional garnishes: chocolate dessert decorations, edible flowers, powdered sugar or unsweetened cocoa powder |

1. Preheat oven to 375°F. Unroll phyllo. Place sugar in **Flour/Sugar Shaker**. Lay one sheet phyllo on flat work surface and spray with nonstick cooking spray. Sprinkle with some of the sugar. Repeat, stacking next two sheets of phyllo on first and using up all of the sugar. Lay fourth sheet on top and spray lightly with cooking spray. Using **Kitchen Shears**, cut phyllo stack into 4 strips and then crosswise into 3 strips, creating 12 squares of layered phyllo dough.

2. Place one square in each cup of **Stoneware Muffin Pan**, arranging slightly to fit cup. Bake 10-12 minutes or until lightly browned. Remove pan from oven and let cool 2 minutes on **Nonstick Cooling Rack**. With tip of **Utility Knife**, carefully remove each phyllo nest; cool completely.

3. Prepare mousse mix with milk in **Classic Batter Bowl** according to package directions, adding Cinnamon to mix; fold in whipped topping. Refrigerate 1-2 hours. When ready to serve, fill **Easy Accent®** **Decorator**, fitted with closed star tip, with mousse mixture and pipe decoratively into each phyllo nest. Garnish with chocolate dessert decorations, edible flowers and a sprinkle of powdered sugar or cocoa powder, if desired.

Yield: 12 servings

LOW FAT  Nutrients per serving (1 nest): Calories 80, Total Fat 2.5 g, Saturated Fat 2 g, Cholesterol 0 mg, Carbohydrate 12 g, Protein 2 g, Sodium 45 mg, Fiber 1 g
Diabetic exchanges per serving (1 nest): 1 Starch (1 Carb)

# Treats that Travel

*Crowd-Pleasing Desserts*
*for Parties, Picnics and Potlucks*

Cookies 'n Cream Cake p. 98

**Prep time:** 15 minutes
**Bake time:** 50-55 minutes
**Cool time:** 1 hour

### Tool Tips

▲ Use the **Egg Separator**, which conveniently fits over the rim of most bowls, to separate the eggs. Cover and refrigerate the yolks to add to your breakfast scrambled eggs.

▲ The **Citrus Peeler** is the perfect tool to aid in loosening cakes from the fluted sides and center tube of the Stoneware Fluted Pan.

▲ The sharp, serrated edges of the **Slice 'N Serve®** allow for easily cutting through cakes and pies for serving. Like many of our cutting tools, it comes with a protective plastic guard for safe storage.

# Cookies 'n Cream Cake

*Pictured on p. 96*
*You'll find this cake ideal for the school's cake walk.*
*Kids, and those who never want to grow up, love this dessert.*

### Cake

| | |
|---|---|
| 12 | creme-filled chocolate sandwich cookies, coarsely chopped |
| 1 | package (18.25 ounces) white cake mix |
| 3/4 | cup water |
| 1/2 | cup sour cream |
| 3 | egg whites |
| 2 | tablespoons vegetable oil |

### Icing

| | |
|---|---|
| 6 | creme-filled chocolate sandwich cookies, coarsely chopped |
| 1 1/2 | cups powdered sugar |
| 1/4 | cup sour cream |
| 3 | tablespoons butter or margarine, softened |

1. Preheat oven to 325°F. Spray **Stoneware Fluted Pan** with nonstick cooking spray. For cake, coarsely chop cookies using **Crinkle Cutter**; set aside. Combine cake mix, water, sour cream, egg whites and oil in **Classic Batter Bowl**; mix according to package directions.

2. Pour half of batter into pan. Sprinkle chopped cookies evenly over top of batter but not touching sides of pan. Spoon remaining batter over cookies.

3. Bake 50-55 minutes or until **Cake Tester** inserted near center of cake comes out clean. Cool in pan 10 minutes. Loosen cake from sides and center tube of pan. Invert onto **Nonstick Cooling Rack**; remove pan. Cool completely.

4. For icing, coarsely chop cookies; set aside. Combine powdered sugar, sour cream and butter in **Small Batter Bowl**; beat until smooth. Ice top of cake allowing some to flow down the sides. Sprinkle top with cookies. Let stand until icing is set. Cut into slices. Store leftover cake, covered, in refrigerator.

Yield: 16 servings

Nutrients per serving: Calories 300, Total Fat 12 g, Saturated Fat 4 g, Cholesterol 15 mg, Carbohydrate 45 g, Protein 3 g, Sodium 330 mg, Fiber less than 1 g
Diabetic exchanges per serving: 1 Starch, 2 Fruit, 2 Fat (3 Carb, 2 Fat)

# Fancy Southern Nut Bars

*Pictured on p. 101*

*Cut these bars small as they're wonderfully rich with nuts, honey and cream.*
*A Stoneware Bar Pan will make enough for your next holiday gathering.*

**Crust**

| | |
|---|---|
| 3/4 | cup butter, softened |
| 1/3 | cup granulated sugar |
| 1 | egg |
| 1/4 | teaspoon salt |
| 2 1/2 | cups all-purpose flour |

**Filling**

| | |
|---|---|
| 1 | can (10 ounces) salted cashews or deluxe mixed nuts, coarsely chopped |
| 1 | cup pecan halves, coarsely chopped |
| 1 | lemon |
| 3/4 | cup butter or margarine |
| 1/2 | cup honey |
| 1 | cup packed brown sugar |
| 1/3 | cup granulated sugar |
| 1/4 | cup whipping cream |

1. Preheat oven to 350°F. For crust, beat butter and sugar until light and fluffy in **Classic Batter Bowl**. Blend in egg and salt. Gradually beat in flour just until mixture holds together. Using fingertips, pat dough over bottom and halfway up sides of **Stoneware Bar Pan**. Roll crust evenly using floured **Baker's Roller™**. Bake 20 minutes. Remove from oven to **Nonstick Cooling Rack**.

2. Meanwhile, for filling, coarsely chop nuts using **Food Chopper**. Using **Lemon Zester/Scorer**, zest lemon. Set nuts and lemon zest aside.

3. Heat butter and honey in **Small (2-qt.) Saucepan** over medium-high heat until butter is melted, stirring occasionally.

4. Add sugars, stirring until dissolved, then bring to a full, rolling boil. Boil 2 minutes without stirring. Remove pan from heat.

5. Immediately stir in cream. Add nuts and zest; stir until nuts are coated. Cool 5 minutes. Spoon filling evenly over hot crust; spread with **Large Spreader**. Bake 10-13 minutes or until center of filling just begins to bubble. (Filling will still look fluid.) Cool completely. Cut into bars. Store in tightly covered container in a cool place.

Yield: 48 bars

Nutrients per serving (1 bar): Calories 170, Total Fat 11 g, Saturated Fat 4.5 g, Cholesterol 20 mg, Carbohydrate 17 g, Protein 2 g, Sodium 115 mg, Fiber less than 1 g
Diabetic exchanges per serving (1 bar): 1 Starch, 2 Fat (1 Carb, 2 Fat)

## Kitchen Tips

Prep time: 50 minutes
Bake time: 10-13 minutes
Cool time: 2 hours

### Cook's Tips

▲ For the best flavor, use butter for these nutty bars.

▲ When forming the crust, pinch off small pieces of dough and place 1-2 inches apart over bottom of Bar Pan. Press the mounds of dough with your fingertips to completely cover bottom and halfway up sides, then make the crust smooth and even with a floured **Baker's Roller™**.

### Tool Tips

▲ For added assurance, you can use the **Digital Thermometer** when preparing the filling. Once the sugar mixture has boiled 2 minutes, it should be at the Firm-Ball Stage (Level 3) or 244°-248°F.

▲ The **Mini-Serving Spatula** is just the right size utensil for removing the cut bars from the pan.

**Prep time:** 45 minutes
**Bake time:** 20-22 minutes
**Cool time:** 45 minutes

### Cook's Tip

▲ To prevent dough from sticking to the **Mini-Tart Shaper**, dip it into flour before making each tart shell.

### Tool Tips

▲ The **Quikut Paring Knife** is a good tool to use when removing tartlets from the pan. Run the thin, narrow blade around the edge of each tartlet before gently lifting from muffin cup.

▲ For quick and easy garnishing, keep a **Flour/Sugar Shaker** filled with powdered sugar on hand. It's great for dusting the tops of cakes, bar cookies and pretty tartlets like these.

# Lemon Tartlets

*Dainty citrus tarts are a sweet addition to any tea table.*
*These have a buttery shell and a custard-like filling.*

**Tart Shells**

| | |
|---|---|
| 1/2 | cup butter or margarine, softened |
| 1/3 | cup granulated sugar |
| 1 | egg white |
| 1 1/4 | cups all-purpose flour |

**Filling**

| | |
|---|---|
| 2 | eggs |
| 1/3 | cup granulated sugar |
| 1 | tablespoon butter or margarine, melted and cooled |
| 1 | large lemon |
| | Powdered sugar (optional) |

1. Preheat oven to 325°F. Spray cups of **Deluxe Mini-Muffin Pan** with nonstick cooking spray. For tart shells, in **Classic Batter Bowl**, beat butter and sugar until light and fluffy. Add egg white; blend well. Add flour; mix just until well blended. Using **Small Scoop**, drop level scoops of dough into muffin cups. Press dough into cups with well-floured **Mini-Tart Shaper**.

2. For filling, lightly whisk eggs in **Small Batter Bowl**. Whisk in sugar and butter. Zest lemon using **Lemon Zester/Scorer**. Finely chop zest to measure 2 teaspoons zest. Add zest and 3 tablespoons lemon juice to Batter Bowl; mix well. Pour filling evenly into tart shells.

3. Bake 20-22 minutes or until edges are light golden brown. Remove pan to **Nonstick Cooling Rack**; cool 5 minutes. Carefully remove tartlets from muffin cups. Cool completely. Store in tightly covered container in refrigerator. Sprinkle with powdered sugar before serving, if desired.

Yield: 24 tartlets

Nutrients per serving (1 tartlet): Calories 90, Total Fat 5 g, Saturated Fat 3 g, Cholesterol 30 mg, Carbohydrate 11 g, Protein 1 g, Sodium 50 mg, Fiber 0 g
Diabetic exchanges per serving (1 tartlet): 1 Fruit, 1 Fat (1 Carb, 1 Fat)

# Black Forest Trifle

*An English-style dessert with all the flavors of a famous German torte makes for an unbeatable combination.*

- 1 package (9 ounces) devil's food cake mix (plus ingredients to make cake)
- 2 bars (1.55 ounces each) milk chocolate candy, divided
- 1 can (30 ounces) cherry pie filling
- 1 teaspoon almond extract
- 1/2 cup cranberry cherry juice
- 2 cups cold milk
- 2 packages (3.3 ounces each) white chocolate instant pudding and pie filling
- 1 container (8 ounces) frozen whipped topping, thawed

1. Preheat oven to 350°F. Cut an 8 1/2-inch square of **Parchment Paper** and lay in bottom of **Square Baker**. Prepare cake mix according to package directions; spread over bottom of Baker. Bake 25 minutes or until **Cake Tester** inserted in center comes out clean. Cool completely.

2. Loosen cake from sides of Baker and invert cake onto **Cutting Board**; remove parchment. Cut cake into 1-inch cubes using **Serrated Bread Knife**; set aside. Chop 1 1/2 of the chocolate bars using **Food Chopper**. Reserve remaining chocolate for garnishing.

3. Combine cherry pie filling and almond extract in **Small Batter Bowl**; remove 1/2 cup for garnishing and set aside. Stir juice into cherry pie filling in Batter Bowl.

4. Pour milk into **Classic Batter Bowl**; whisk in pudding mixes until mixture begins to thicken. Fold in whipped topping.

5. To assemble trifle, place half of the cake cubes in bottom of **Chillzanne® Bowl**. Layer half of the cherry pie filling mixture evenly over cake cubes. Sprinkle with half of the chopped chocolate; top with half of the pudding mixture, pressing lightly. Repeat layers.

6. Garnish top of trifle with reserved cherry pie filling and chocolate curls made with reserved chocolate. Refrigerate at least 30 minutes before serving.

Yield: 10 servings

Nutrients per serving: Calories 420, Total Fat 11 g, Saturated Fat 8 g, Cholesterol 20 mg, Carbohydrate 75 g, Protein 4 g, Sodium 520 mg, Fiber 1 g
Diabetic exchanges per serving: 1 Starch, 4 Fruit, 2 Fat (5 Carb, 1 Fat)

## Kitchen Tips

Prep time: 30 minutes
Bake time: 25 minutes
Cool time: 30 minutes
Chill time: 30 minutes

### Make Ahead Tip

▲ This trifle can be assembled several hours before serving, or even the night before.

### Tool Tips

▲ To make chocolate curls, hold the **Vegetable Peeler** across the short side of the milk chocolate bar. Using even pressure, push the blade away from you to create curls. Or, grate chocolate over dessert using the **Deluxe Cheese Grater**.

▲ Our unique **Chillzanne® Bowl** is great for taking foods to picnics and potlucks because it keeps foods cold for hours. Place it upright in the freezer about four hours before assembling trifle to allow the unique food-safe gel within the bowl's sides plenty of time to freeze.

**Prep time:** 10 minutes
**Bake time:** 36-38 minutes
**Cool time:** 1 hour

### Cook's Tips

▲ To melt butter, place in the **Small Micro-Cooker®**. Microwave on HIGH 1 minute or until melted.

▲ To set the chocolate-peanut butter mixture faster, place the pan of chocolate-topped brownies in the refrigerator for 20 minutes or until set.

### Tool Tip

▲ The **Handy Scraper** is perfect for transferring chopped ingredients, like the peanuts in this recipe, from the **Cutting Board** to the Batter Bowl.

# Triple Layer Brownies

*Nothing satisfies more than fudgy brownies topped with melted chocolate and peanut butter on a chewy peanutty crust. Your friends will love them.*

½ cup dry roasted peanuts, chopped
1 cup quick or old-fashioned oats
½ cup packed brown sugar
⅓ cup all-purpose flour
¼ teaspoon baking soda
½ cup butter or margarine, melted
1 package (19-21 ounces) fudge brownie mix (plus ingredients to make brownies)
¾ cup semi-sweet chocolate morsels
½ cup creamy peanut butter
Additional chopped peanuts (optional)

1. Preheat oven to 350°F. Spray **Rectangular Baker** with nonstick cooking spray. Chop peanuts using **Food Chopper**. Combine oats, brown sugar, flour, baking soda and peanuts in **Small Batter Bowl**. Add butter; mix well. Press oat mixture onto bottom of Baker. Bake 8 minutes. Remove from oven.

2. Meanwhile, prepare brownie mix according to package directions. Gently spoon batter over partially baked crust; carefully spread to edges of Baker. Bake according to package directions for brownies (28-30 minutes). Cool completely.

3. Combine chocolate morsels and peanut butter in **Small Micro-Cooker®**. Microwave, uncovered, on HIGH 1 minute. Stir until smooth. Spread chocolate mixture evenly over cooled brownies using **Large Spreader**. Sprinkle with additional chopped peanuts, if desired. Cool until chocolate mixture is set. Cut into bars. Store in tightly covered container in refrigerator.

Yield: 32 bars

Nutrients per serving (1 bar): Calories 220, Total Fat 13 g, Saturated Fat 4 g, Cholesterol 20 mg, Carbohydrate 24 g, Protein 3 g, Sodium 115 mg, Fiber less than 1 g
Diabetic exchanges per serving: 1 Starch, ½ Fruit, 2 Fat (1½ Carb, 2 Fat)

# Strawberry Margarita Squares

*This dessert may seem familiar, but with a fun flavor twist,*
*we think it's never been so refreshing.*

## Crust

- 2 cups (66) fat-free mini-twist pretzels (1 cup crushed)
- 1/2 cup butter or margarine, melted
- 1/4 cup sugar

## Filling

- 2 packages (8 ounces each) cream cheese, softened
- 1/2 cup thawed, frozen margarita mix concentrate (non-alcoholic)
- 2 containers (8 ounces each) frozen whipped topping, thawed, divided
- 1 package (3 ounces) strawberry gelatin
- 1/2 cup boiling water
- 1 package (10 ounces) frozen sliced strawberries in syrup
  Fresh strawberry slices (optional)
  Lime slices (optional)

1. Preheat oven to 350°F. For crust, finely crush pretzels in resealable plastic bag with **Baker's Roller™**. Melt butter in **Small Micro-Cooker®** on HIGH 30 seconds or until melted. Add crushed pretzels and sugar; mix well. Press mixture onto bottom of **Rectangular Baker**. Bake 10 minutes. Cool completely.

2. For filling, beat cream cheese and margarita mix in **Classic Batter Bowl** until well blended. Fold in 2 cups of the whipped topping. Using **Large Spreader**, carefully spread cream cheese mixture evenly over crust. Refrigerate while preparing strawberry layer.

3. Place gelatin in **Small Batter Bowl**. Stir in boiling water; stir until completely dissolved. Add frozen strawberries and stir until strawberries separate and gelatin is thickened (a spoon drawn through mixture will leave an impression). Whisk in 3 cups of the whipped topping using **Stainless Steel Whisk**. Pour over cream cheese layer, spreading to edges. Refrigerate 3 hours to set.

4. Cut dessert into 15 squares. Garnish each serving with remaining whipped topping using **Easy Accent® Decorator**. Top with fresh strawberry and lime slices, if desired.

Yield: 15 servings

Nutrients per serving: Calories 330, Total Fat 23 g, Saturated Fat 16 g, Cholesterol 50 mg, Carbohydrate 26 g, Protein 3 g, Sodium 250 mg, Fiber 0 g
Diabetic exchanges per serving: 1 Starch, 1 Fruit, 4 Fat (2 Carb, 4 Fat)

## Kitchen Tips

Prep time: 45 minutes
Bake time: 10 minutes
Cool time: 30 minutes
Chill time: 3 hours

### Cook's Tips

▲ Frozen margarita mix concentrate is available in 10-ounce cans in the frozen juice section of your supermarket. Reserve remaining concentrate to make this dessert again, or reconstitute with 2 1/2 cups water. Add sugar to taste and serve over ice for a refreshing beverage.

▲ This dessert is best if made early on the day of serving. The pretzel crust can become soggy if the dessert is made too far in advance. Plan to serve it at a large gathering, as leftovers won't hold well.

### Tool Tip

▲ If any of the strawberries stay frozen in clumps, cut with the **Kitchen Shears** and continue stirring until separated.

*While Red Velvet Cake is best known in the South, the festive color of these chocolate cupcakes will bring out the smiles anywhere.*

## Kitchen Tips

**Prep time:** 15 minutes
**Bake time:** 18-22 minutes per batch
**Cool time:** 30 minutes

### Cook's Tips

▲ If you don't have buttermilk on hand, you can substitute sour milk. Add 1 tablespoon plus 1 teaspoon white vinegar or lemon juice to enough milk to make 1 1/3 cups; let stand 5 minutes.

▲ Vegetable shortening is available in cans or sticks. Use regular, not butter flavor, for the whitest frosting. It's easy to measure in the **Measure-All® Cup**. In a hurry? A canned fluffy white frosting can be substituted for the scratch recipe.

▲ Tote these cupcakes to the picnic on our **Chillzanne® Platter**. There's no need to chill the platter first. Just place the decorated cupcakes on the platter, cover with the lid and snap on the handle.

### Cupcakes

- 1 package (18.25 ounces) devil's food cake mix
- 1 1/3 cups buttermilk
- 1/2 cup vegetable oil
- 3 eggs
- 2 tablespoons red food coloring

### Frosting & Decorations

- 1/2 cup solid vegetable shortening
- 1/2 teaspoon almond or vanilla extract
- 2 cups powdered sugar
- 2 tablespoons milk
  Colored sprinkles, decors or chopped nuts (optional)

1. Preheat oven to 350°F. Place paper liners in cups of **Stoneware Muffin Pan**. For cupcakes, combine cake mix, buttermilk, oil, eggs and food coloring in **Classic Batter Bowl**; mix according to package directions.

2. Using **Large Scoop**, drop heaping scoops of batter into 12 muffin cups (half of batter will be remaining). Bake 18-22 minutes or until **Cake Tester** inserted near center comes out clean. Cool cupcakes in pan 5 minutes; remove to **Nonstick Cooling Rack**. Cool completely. Repeat with paper liners and remaining batter.

3. For frosting, beat shortening and almond extract until well blended. Slowly add 1 cup of the powdered sugar; beat well. Add 1 tablespoon of the milk. Gradually beat in remaining powdered sugar and milk to make a spreading consistency. Frost tops of cupcakes using **All-Purpose Spreader**. Decorate as desired.

Yield: 24 cupcakes

Nutrients per serving (1 cupcake): Calories 220, Total Fat 12 g, Saturated Fat 2.5 g, Cholesterol 40 mg, Carbohydrate 26 g, Protein 3 g, Sodium 207 mg, Fiber 0 g
Diabetic exchanges per serving (1 cupcake): 1 Starch, 1 Fruit, 2 Fat (2 Carb, 2 Fat)

# Apricot Linzer Bars

*If it's your turn to bring the office treats, these old-world,*
*spicy fruit bars are just the right thing.*

1¼  cups all-purpose flour
1¼  cups powdered sugar
½  teaspoon Pantry Cinnamon Plus™
    Spice Blend
¾  cup walnuts, finely grated
½  cup butter or margarine, melted
1  small orange
⅔  cup apricot preserves

1. Preheat oven to 375°F. Mix flour, powdered sugar and Spice Blend in **Classic Batter Bowl**. Grate walnuts into Batter Bowl using **Deluxe Cheese Grater** fitted with small grating drum.

2. Microwave butter in **Small Micro-Cooker®** on HIGH 30-45 seconds or until melted. Using **Lemon Zester/Scorer**, zest orange with short strokes to measure 1½ teaspoons zest. Add butter and orange zest to Batter Bowl; mix until crumbly. Reserve ¾ cup crumb mixture. Press remaining crumb mixture onto bottom of **Square Baker**.

3. Spread preserves over crust to within ¼ inch of edge using **All-Purpose Spreader**. Sprinkle with reserved crumb mixture, pressing gently into preserves.

4. Bake 27-32 minutes or until preserves are bubbly and top is golden brown. Cool completely. Cut into bars. Store covered at room temperature.

Yield: 24 bars

Nutrients per serving (1 bar): Calories 120, Total Fat 6 g, Saturated Fat 2.5 g, Cholesterol 10 mg, Carbohydrate 17 g, Protein 1 g, Sodium 45 mg, Fiber 0 g
Diabetic exchanges per serving (1 bar): 1 Starch, 1 Fat (1 Carb, 1 Fat)

## Kitchen Tips

Prep time: 15 minutes
Bake time: 27-32 minutes
Cool time: 2 hours

### Cook's Tips

▲ It's easy to cut these bar cookies into triangles. First, cut into 16 squares, then cut each square diagonally in half to make 32 triangles.

▲ Pumpkin pie spice or ground cinnamon can be substituted for Cinnamon Plus™ Spice Blend, if desired.

### Tool Tip

▲ If preserves contain large pieces of apricot, use the **Kitchen Shears** to snip the fruit pieces more finely.

### Cook's Tips

▲ For a different flavored dip, try substituting light sugar-free apricot or raspberry preserves or orange marmalade for the strawberry preserves.

▲ Dip peaches, bananas, apples and pears in lemon juice to prevent browning.

▲ To make fruit kabobs, arrange cut-up fruits on long wooden skewers.

### Tool Tips

▲ The convenient, snap-on **Chillzanne® Platter Handle** lets you easily carry your fresh fruit platter anywhere.

▲ When traveling a distance, especially during warm weather months, transport dip in a **Chillzanne® Mini-Bowl** to keep it well chilled before spooning it into the bowl of the Divider.

# Summer Fruit Sampler

*A colorful fruit platter adds sparkle to any buffet table and is the perfect dessert for those people on low fat, low-calorie diets.*

**Fruit Platter**

8 cups assorted fresh fruit such as whole strawberries; sliced kiwi, peaches or banana; cantaloupe, honeydew or pineapple chunks; apple or pear wedges; or grapes

**Dip**

1 orange
½ cup reduced-fat sour cream
¼ cup light sugar-free strawberry preserves
1½ cups thawed, frozen light whipped topping

1. For fruit platter, prepare and arrange fruit on **Chillzanne® Platter** fitted with **Divider** (see *Creating Fancy Fruit*, at right). Cover with lid and refrigerate until ready to serve.

2. For dip, zest orange with **Lemon Zester/Scorer**. Finely chop zest to measure 2 teaspoons.

3. In **Small Batter Bowl**, combine sour cream, preserves and orange zest. Fold in whipped topping until combined. Cover and refrigerate until ready to use.

4. To serve, spoon dip into center bowl of Chillzanne® Platter Divider. Serve using **Large Serving Tongs**.

Yield: 16 servings

### Creating Fancy Fruit

Strawberries: Slice up to hulls using **Egg Slicer Plus®**; gently spread slices slightly apart to create fans.

Kiwi: Cut peeled kiwi using **Crinkle Cutter®**.

Peaches or nectarines: Cut fruit in half; remove pit. Slice into smaller wedges using **Utility Knife**.

Bananas: Slice diagonally into 1-inch pieces using **Crinkle Cutter**.

Melons: Remove melon from rind; cut into chunks using **Crinkle Cutter**. Or, scoop melon balls with **Small Scoop**.

Apples and pears: Cut into wedges using **Apple Wedger**.

*LOW FAT* Nutrients per serving (½ cup fruit and 2 tablespoons dip): Calories 60, Total Fat 1.5 g, Saturated Fat 1 g, Cholesterol less than 5 mg, Carbohydrate 12 g, Protein 1 g, Sodium 10 mg, Fiber 1 g
Diabetic exchanges per serving: 1 Fruit (1 Carb)

# S'Mores Galore

*Based on a favorite gooey treat made 'round the campfire, we think these bars will go over big at the next slumber party—served 'round the fireplace hearth, of course.*

20 whole (about 5 x 2-inches) honey graham crackers, divided

6 bars (1.55 ounces each) milk chocolate candy, coarsely chopped

1 package (16 ounces) miniature marshmallows, divided

6 tablespoons butter or margarine, divided

3 tablespoons milk

1. Preheat oven to 350°F. Arrange a single layer of graham crackers to completely cover bottom of **Stoneware Bar Pan**, breaking crackers to fit. Toast in oven 2 minutes. Remove pan to **Nonstick Cooling Rack**.

2. Coarsely break remaining graham crackers into large **Colander Bowl**; set aside. Coarsely chop chocolate bars using **Food Chopper**; set aside.

3. Combine 3 cups of the marshmallows, 3 tablespoons of the butter and milk in **Small Micro-Cooker®**. Microwave on HIGH 1 minute. Stir until smooth. Add half of the chopped chocolate; stir until chocolate is completely melted. Using **Large Spreader**, spread marshmallow mixture evenly over graham crackers in pan.

4. Melt remaining 3 tablespoons butter; toss with broken graham crackers. Add remaining marshmallows and chopped chocolate; toss lightly. Using **Mix 'N Scraper®**, spoon evenly over mixture in pan. Bake 8-10 minutes or until marshmallows are lightly browned. Cool 15 minutes. Cut into bars. Serve warm or cool.

Yield: 24 bars

Nutrients per serving (1 bar): Calories 200, Total Fat 8 g, Saturated Fat 4 g, Cholesterol 10 mg, Carbohydrate 32 g, Protein 2 g, Sodium 120 mg, Fiber less than 1 g
Diabetic exchanges per serving (1 bar): 1 Starch, 1 Fruit, 1 Fat (2 Carb, 1 Fat)

## Kitchen Tips

**Prep time: 15 minutes**
**Bake time: 10-12 minutes**
**Cool time: 15 minutes**

### Cook's Tips

▲ To arrange a single layer of graham crackers in the Bar Pan, use 12 graham crackers to make two rows in the pan. Break one additional graham cracker lengthwise and add to cover bottom of pan.

▲ These sweet snacks are best when eaten the day they're made. Although you can store them in a tightly covered container, the graham crackers tend to lose their crispness after a day.

▲ To easily cut the S'Mores bars, dip the **Utility Knife** into hot water occasionally while cutting.

Prep time: 20 minutes
Bake time: 25 minutes
Cool time: 45 minutes
Chill time: 1 hour

### Cook's Tips

▲ A cream puff pastry (also called choux paste or pâte à choux) makes the special crust for this dessert. During baking, the eggs cause the crust to puff irregularly. Once cooled, the crust is spread with a creamy vanilla filling and the top of the dessert is smooth and even.

▲ Chocolate will melt quicker when chopped into smaller pieces. Use the **Crinkle Cutter** to coarsely chop the chocolate squares before melting.

### Tool Tip

▲ To release the steam created in the cream puff during baking, prick the surface using the **Hold 'N Slice™**. This handy tool can also be used for pricking pastries and pie crusts.

# Cream Puff Squares

*Make this dessert in our glazed Rectangular Baker
for the next family gathering.*

### Crust
- ¾ **cup water**
- 6 **tablespoons butter or margarine**
- ¾ **cup all-purpose flour**
- 3 **eggs**

### Filling & Topping
- 2 **cups cold milk**
- 2 **packages (3.4 ounces each) vanilla instant pudding and pie filling**
- 1 **container (8 ounces) frozen whipped topping, thawed, divided**
- 2 **squares (1 ounce each) semi-sweet chocolate for baking, chopped**

1. Preheat oven to 400°F. For crust, heat water and butter in **Small (2-qt.) Saucepan** over medium-high heat until butter is melted and mixture comes to a boil. Stir in flour all at once using **Bamboo Spoon**. Reduce heat to low and stir mixture vigorously about 1 minute or until mixture leaves sides of pan and forms a ball. Remove pan from heat; let stand 5 minutes.

2. Add eggs, one at a time, beating after each addition until mixture is smooth. Spread mixture evenly over bottom of **Rectangular Baker** using **Large Spreader**. Bake 20 minutes. (Surface will puff unevenly.) Prick 10-12 times to release steam; continue baking 5 minutes or until crust is golden brown. Cool completely.

3. For filling, pour milk into **Classic Batter Bowl**. Add pudding mixes; whisk 2 minutes until thickened. Fold in 2 cups of the whipped topping. Spread mixture evenly over cooled crust. Refrigerate 1 hour.

4. For topping, place chocolate and remaining whipped topping in **Small Micro-Cooker®**. Microwave, uncovered, on HIGH 30-40 seconds; stir until smooth. Pour chocolate mixture into small, resealable plastic bag. Close bag. Cut dessert into 15 squares. Cut off the very tip of one corner of the plastic bag with **Kitchen Shears**. Garnish each serving with a drizzle of chocolate. Refrigerate until ready to serve or serve immediately.

Yield: 15 servings

Nutrients per serving: Calories 200, Total Fat 11 g, Saturated Fat 7 g, Cholesterol 55 mg, Carbohydrate 24 g, Protein 3 g, Sodium 260 mg, Fiber 0 g
Diabetic exchanges per serving: 1 Starch, ½ Fruit, 2 Fat (1½ Carb, 2 Fat)

# Snazzy Snickerdoodles

*Let The Pampered Chef Cookie Press
put an end to ho-hum cookie shapes.*

1³/4 cups all-purpose flour
  1 teaspoon cream of tartar
¹/2 teaspoon baking soda
¹/8 teaspoon salt
¹/2 cup butter or margarine, softened
  1 cup plus 2 tablespoons sugar, divided
  1 egg
  1 teaspoon vanilla
  1 teaspoon Pantry Korintje Cinnamon

1. Preheat oven to 375°F. Combine flour, cream of tartar, baking soda and salt in **Small Batter Bowl**; mix well and set aside. In **Classic Batter Bowl**, mix butter and 1 cup of the sugar until well blended and creamy using **Bamboo Spoon**. Stir in egg and vanilla. Add flour mixture, stirring until soft dough forms; do not refrigerate.

2. Combine remaining 2 tablespoons sugar and Cinnamon in **Flour/Sugar Shaker**. Fill **Cookie Press** fitted with disk #2, #4 or #5 with dough. Press dough onto flat **Baking Stone**, 1 inch apart. Sprinkle cookies generously with sugar-cinnamon mixture.

3. Bake 9-11 minutes or until cookies are set. Remove immediately to **Nonstick Cooling Rack**. Cool completely. Repeat with remaining dough.

Yield: About 3 dozen cookies

LOW FAT | Nutrients per serving (1 cookie): Calories 70, Total Fat 3 g, Saturated Fat 1.5 g, Cholesterol 15 mg, Carbohydrate 11 g, Protein 1 g, Sodium 55 mg, Fiber 0 g
Diabetic exchanges per serving (1 cookie): 1 Fruit, ¹/2 Fat (1 Carb, ¹/2 Fat)

## Kitchen Tips

**Prep time:** 20 minutes
**Bake time:** 9-11 minutes per batch
**Cool time:** 15 minutes

### Cook's Tips

▲ Cream of tartar is a traditional ingredient in Snickerdoodles and can be found in the spice section of the grocery store. In a pinch, substitute 1¹/2 teaspoons baking powder for the cream of tartar *and* the baking soda in this recipe.

▲ Ground cinnamon can be substituted for the Korintje Cinnamon, if desired.

▲ This cookie dough will adhere to a warm Baking Stone, so it's not necessary to cool the Stone between batches. You can bake your cookies on **Parchment Paper** for easier cleanup, if you prefer.

### Tool Tip

▲ Before trying the **Cookie Press** for the first time, it's very helpful to read the Use and Care Card.

Prep time: 15 minutes
Bake time: 22-25 minutes
Cool time: 30 minutes

## Cook's Tips

▲ In a pinch, sour milk can be substituted for buttermilk. Combine 1/2 cup milk with 1 1/2 teaspoons vinegar or lemon juice. Let stand 5 minutes or until slightly thickened before using.

▲ The cake needs to be warm for the frosting to be of correct spreading consistency. Cool cake just 10 minutes before topping it with the frosting.

# Texas Sheet Cake

*Not just Texans can appreciate the big, delicious flavor of these Bar Pan treats. With some reduced-fat ingredients, we've even lightened them up a bit for y'all.*

## Cake

- 2 cups all-purpose flour
- 2 cups sugar
- 1 cup water
- 1/2 cup (1 stick) vegetable oil spread (70% fat)
- 1/4 cup unsweetened cocoa powder
- 2 eggs
- 1/2 cup buttermilk
- 1 teaspoon baking soda
- 1 teaspoon vanilla
- 1/2 teaspoon salt

## Frosting

- 5 tablespoons fat-free (skim) milk
- 1/4 cup unsweetened cocoa powder
- 2 tablespoons vegetable oil spread (70% fat)
- 3 cups powdered sugar
- 1 teaspoon vanilla

1. Preheat oven to 350°F. Spray **Stoneware Bar Pan** with nonstick cooking spray. For cake, combine flour and sugar in **Small Batter Bowl**; set aside. In **Medium (3-qt.) Saucepan**, heat water, vegetable oil spread and cocoa powder over medium heat; bring to a boil, stirring occasionally. Using **Nylon Spiral Whisk**, stir in flour mixture. Add eggs, buttermilk, baking soda, vanilla and salt; mix well. Pour into pan.

2. Bake 22-25 minutes or until **Cake Tester** inserted in center comes out clean. Remove from oven to **Nonstick Cooling Rack**. Cool 10 minutes before frosting.

3. For frosting, place milk, cocoa powder and vegetable oil spread in **Large Micro-Cooker®**. Microwave on HIGH 45 seconds or until spread is melted; whisk until smooth. Add powdered sugar and vanilla; whisk until smooth. Spread over warm cake using **Large Spreader**. Cool completely. Cut into squares. Store in tightly covered container in refrigerator.

Yield: 24 squares

Nutrients per serving (1 square): Calories 210, Total Fat 5 g, Saturated Fat 1 g, Cholesterol 20 mg, Carbohydrate 41 g, Protein 2 g, Sodium 160 mg, Fiber less than 1 g
Diabetic exchanges per serving (1 square): 1 Starch, 2 Fruit, 1 Fat (3 Carb, 1 Fat)

*Variation:* **Tex-Mex Sheet Cake:** Add 1 teaspoon **Pantry Korintje Cinnamon** (or ground cinnamon) to the flour-sugar mixture. Proceed as recipe directs.

# Coffee House Cookies

*Indulge in a giant decadent cookie and a cup of
The Pampered Chef's Good Company™ Coffee.*

1½ cups all-purpose flour
½ teaspoon baking soda
¼ teaspoon salt
½ cup butter or margarine, softened
¾ cup packed brown sugar
1 egg
1 teaspoon vanilla
1 cup coarsely chopped walnuts or
   pecans, divided
1 cup semi-sweet chocolate chunks,
   divided
2 bars (1.5-2 ounces each) favorite
   chocolate candy (see Cook's Tip)

1. Preheat oven to 350°F. Combine flour, baking soda and salt in **Small Batter Bowl**; mix well. In **Classic Batter Bowl**, beat butter and brown sugar until creamy. Add egg and vanilla; beat well. Gradually beat in flour mixture.

2. Stir ⅔ cup of the nuts and ⅔ cup of the chocolate chunks into dough. Cut candy bars into small pieces, about the size of chocolate chunks; set aside.

3. Using **Large Scoop**, drop 6 level scoops of dough, 3 inches apart, onto **Rectangle Stone**. (Cookies will spread while baking.) Flatten scoops slightly with palm of hand. Lightly press half of the remaining nuts, chocolate and candy into tops of cookies.

4. Bake 14-16 minutes or until cookies are almost set. (Centers will be soft. Do not overbake.) Cool 7 minutes on Baking Stone. Using **Large Serving Spatula**, remove cookies to **Nonstick Cooling Rack**. Cool completely. Repeat with remaining dough.

Yield: 1 dozen cookies

Nutrients per serving (1 cookie): Calories 360, Total Fat 20 g, Saturated Fat 6 g, Cholesterol 40 mg, Carbohydrate 40 g, Protein 5 g, Sodium 210 mg, Fiber 2 g
Diabetic exchanges per serving (1 cookie): 2 Starch, 1 Fruit, 3½ Fat (3 Carb, 3½ Fat)

*Variation:* **Coffee House Bar Cookies:**
Double all ingredients and use 1 package (11.5 ounces) semi-sweet chocolate chunks. Prepare dough as recipe directs, stirring 1⅓ cups of the chopped nuts and 1⅓ cups of the chocolate chunks into dough. Using **Large Spreader**, spread dough in **Stoneware Bar Pan**. Lightly press remaining ingredients into top of dough. Bake at 350°F for 20-23 minutes or until golden brown. Cool completely in pan. Cut into bars.

Yield: 32 bars

Prep time: 20 minutes
Bake time: 10-12 minutes
Cool/Chill time: 1 hour

## Cook's Tips

▲ Once the chocolate is firm, store *Confetti Crisps* in a tightly covered container in a cool place at room temperature so they will stay crisp.

▲ Colorful miniature baking bits are available in semi-sweet or milk chocolate flavors. Either is fine for this recipe.

## Tool Tip

▲ If you like, you can be confident your sugar mixture has boiled long enough by using the **Digital Thermometer** and heating the mixture to 244°F (Level 3). Otherwise, be sure to time the 4-minute boiling period carefully.

# Confetti Crisps

*Topped with crispy, crunchy and colorful ingredients,*
*these treats will be a hit at any bake sale.*

| | |
|---|---|
| 40 | square (about 2 inches) saltine crackers |
| 3/4 | cup packed brown sugar |
| 3/4 | cup butter (do not use margarine) |
| 1 | teaspoon vanilla |
| 1 | cup semi-sweet chocolate morsels |
| 1 | cup mini-twist pretzels, broken into small pieces |
| 1/3 | cup chopped peanuts |
| 1/3 | cup candy-coated chocolate miniature baking bits |
| 1/3 | cup raisins (optional) |

1. Preheat oven to 350°F. Arrange crackers side by side in single layer in **Stoneware Bar Pan**.

2. Combine brown sugar, butter and vanilla in **Small (2-qt.) Saucepan**. Cook over medium heat, stirring occasionally with **Nylon Spiral Whisk**, until mixture comes to a full boil across the surface. Boil, stirring constantly, 4 minutes.

3. Immediately pour sugar mixture over crackers and spread evenly with **Large Spreader**. Bake 10-12 minutes or until bubbly and lightly browned. Remove pan from oven to **Nonstick Cooling Rack**.

4. Immediately sprinkle baked crackers with chocolate morsels. Let stand 3 minutes, allowing morsels to soften, then spread evenly over surface. Sprinkle with pretzels, peanuts, baking bits and raisins, if desired. Lightly press toppings into melted chocolate using back of **Large Serving Spatula**. Let stand at room temperature to cool completely. Refrigerate 20 minutes to firm chocolate. Cut into squares.

Yield: 40 squares

Nutrients per serving (1 square): Calories 100, Total Fat 6 g, Saturated Fat 3 g, Cholesterol 10 mg, Carbohydrate 11 g, Protein less than 1 g, Sodium 90 mg, Fiber 0 g
Diabetic exchanges per serving (1 square): 1 Fruit, 1 Fat (1 Carb, 1 Fat)

# Index

## About Our Recipes

All recipes were developed and tested in The Pampered Chef Test Kitchens by professional home economists. For best results, we recommend you use the ingredients indicated in the recipe. The preparation and baking times at the beginning of each recipe serve as a helpful guide when planning your time in the kitchen. As an important first step, we suggest you read through the recipe and assemble the necessary ingredients and equipment. "Prep time" is the approximate amount of time needed to prepare recipe ingredients before a final "Bake time." Prep time includes active steps such as chopping and mixing. It can also include cooking ingredients for a dessert that is assembled and then baked. Some preparation steps can be done simultaneously or during cooking and are usually indicated by the term "meanwhile." Some recipes that have steps not easily separated have a combined "Prep and bake (or cook) time."

## A Note on Nutrition

The nutrition information in *Delightful Desserts* can help you decide how specific recipes can fit into your overall meal plan. At the end of each recipe, we list calories, total fat, saturated fat, cholesterol, carbohydrate, protein, sodium and fiber. We also include diabetic exchange information commonly used by people with diabetes. This information is based on the 1995 *Exchange Lists for Meal Planning* by the American Diabetes Association and the American Dietetic Association. For each recipe, two lists of exchanges are provided. The first option is based on the traditional method of figuring diabetic exchanges; the second option is given in parentheses and reflects the newer system of carbohydrate counting. If you use the exchanges, consult your doctor, certified diabetes educator or registered dietitian.

Nutritional analysis for each recipe is based on the first ingredient listed whenever a choice is given and does not include optional ingredients, garnishes, fat used to grease pans or serving suggestions. The ingredients used in our recipes and for nutritional analyses are based on most commonly purchased foods and unless indicated otherwise use 2 percent reduced-fat milk and large eggs. When margarine is an ingredient option, use a product containing 80 percent fat and not vegetable oil spread. Recipes labeled as LOW FAT have 3 grams or less fat per serving.

## Metric Conversion Chart

| Volume Measurements (dry) | Volume Measurements (fluid) | Dimensions |
|---|---|---|
| ⅛ teaspoon = 0.6 mL | 1 fluid ounce (2 tablespoons) = 30 mL | ⅛ inch = 3 mm |
| ¼ teaspoon = 1.25 mL | 4 fluid ounces (½ cup) = 125 mL | ¼ inch = 6 mm |
| ½ teaspoon = 2.5 mL | 8 fluid ounces (1 cup) = 250 mL | ½ inch = 1 cm |
| ¾ teaspoon = 3.75 mL | 12 fluid ounces (1½ cups) = 375 mL | ¾ inch = 2 cm |
| 1 teaspoon = 5 mL | 16 fluid ounces (2 cups) = 500 mL | 1 inch = 2.5 cm |
| 1 tablespoon = 15 mL | | |
| 2 tablespoons = 30 mL | **Weights (mass)** | **Oven Temperatures** |
| ¼ cup = 50 mL | 1 ounce = 30 g | 250°F = 120°C |
| ⅓ cup = 75 mL | 4 ounces = 125 g | 275°F = 140°C |
| ½ cup = 125 mL | 8 ounces = 250 g | 300°F = 150°C |
| ⅔ cup = 150 mL | 12 ounces = 350 g | 325°F = 160°C |
| ¾ cup = 175 mL | 16 ounces = 1 pound = 500 g | 350°F = 180°C |
| 1 cup = 250 mL | | 375°F = 190°C |
| | | 400°F = 200°C |
| Recipes in this cookbook have not been tested using metric measures. When converting and preparing recipes with metric measures, some variations in quality may be noticed. | | 425°F = 220°C |
| | | 450°F = 230°C |